SABBATICAL from "YES"

*Reconnect with Your Inner Wisdom, Energy and
Creative Fire through 30 Days of Putting Yourself First*

BY CHRISTI DANIELS

ISBN: 978-0-692-29378-2

Printed in the United States of America

"My Sabbatical changed my life! Your class changed my life! This book will definitely change lives!"

"Christi has an amazing ability to research and synthesize years of information gathering it down to one life-changing course - and present it in a fun way. This book should be every woman's 'Bible.'"

"Christi Daniels has all the right answers when it comes to teaching women how to take care of themselves. This book is a bright light beckoning to every woman who has lost herself by putting other people's needs before her own. Christi shows women the way to gracefully and lovingly bring themselves back to their true and full selves. A must read for women of all ages everywhere."

To Hailey, Brett, Avery and Eric
in gratitude for your willingness to be
resilient co-experimenters and forever
residing in my heart.

And to everyone who has ever compromised who they are
to fit into their circumstances. May we each find our way
back to our truest Selves, live from our highest desires and
be so full of ourselves that the world sees, understands and
accepts what a beauty it is to behold.

"There are two basic motivating forces:
fear and love.

When we are afraid, we pull back from life. When
we are in love, we open to all that life has to offer
with passion, excitement, and acceptance. We need
to learn to love ourselves first, in all our glory and our
imperfections. If we cannot love ourselves, we cannot
fully open to our ability to love others or our potential
to create. Evolution and all hopes for a better world
rest in the fearlessness and open-hearted vision of
people who embrace life."

JOHN LENNON

CONTENTS

HOW TO USE THIS BOOK

---

*"The clearest path to happiness emerges
when what you think, what you say
and what you do are in harmony."*

MAHATMA GHANDI

The book you're holding was lovingly prepared for you and is an excerpt of the first two modules in the ten-week program, *Self-Full Living.*™ It's designed to provide you with a step-by-step process that fits right into your daily life and once setup, can be completed within 30 days.

The best way to approach this book is with a sense of curiosity, a willingness to discover something new and an open heart. The *Sabbatical from "Yes"* is an experience that will give you the opportunity to reconnect with the core of who you are, with your dreams and desires by removing your dependence on the expectations of others to dictate your value. To reawaken a sense of aliveness, strength and confidence within you. Each step will give you the opportunity to integrate the work more fully and make your experience more fluid. The steps and chapters are sequential, so please use them in order they were written.

I'll be your guide every step of the way offering context, experiments and exercises. Some of them are unconventional and won't appeal to your logical mind, but I'll ask you to trust me ... it's all part of the plan and it's completely by design. Nothing will happen here for you unless you take action, do the exercises and experiment with it in the laboratory of your life. You can give yourself permission to write in this book, it's yours, but if you prefer more elbow room or would like to make doing the exercises as easy as possible, download the printable workbook that accompanies this book and access audio instructions for each exercise. **www.christidaniels.com/goodies**

To satisfy an element of curiosity, here's a sneak peek of what you will find inside the following pages:

Preparing for Your Sabbatical - Gain clarity about your current life situation and which commitments are energizing or depleting you. Make decisions to keep those aspects that are energizing and either modify or release those that deplete you. Brainstorm your action steps in preparation for taking your *Sabbatical from "Yes."*

Launching Your Sabbatical - Give yourself an official period of rest from the expectations of others by instituting your *Sabbatical from "Yes."* Experience a greater sense of ease, grace and higher levels of energy in your life.

30-Day Action Guide - Call forth your true self one day and one action step at a time. Each week you'll have a specific concept to focus on and an action step to activate the concept. You'll also have reflection questions where you can document your observations from that week and enhance your ability to turn down the volume of the external world while you turn up the volume coming from your inner wisdom.

And with that, let's dive into the book.

INTRODUCTION

"You are the only person who thinks in your mind! You are the power and authority in your world."

LOUISE HAY

Do you ever second guess yourself and look up the definition of words you already know, just to make sure you really do have their understanding correct? I find myself doing this often and it always gives me more clarity and confidence when using the chosen word. As the time to publish this book came closer, I felt that familiar tug to look up the word "sabbatical" to see if there were any new insights that might help frame this experience for you.

The word sabbatical has roots that extend back in history to the Latin word sabbaticus (to cease), from Greek sabbatikos (of the Sabbath) and the Hebrew word shabbat (release). The word sabbath referred to a rest or break from work in seven day or year cycles, such as biblical references in Genesis of God resting on the seventh day and in Mosaic law for letting the land lay fallow every seven years. The Jewish Torah also mandated seven year cycles of debt forgiveness and for granting freedom to slaves. These ancient ways of honoring essential cycles, of balancing effort with rest, starting with stopping, gaining with releasing, were integrated into the work, religious and agricultural practices of the time. Observance of the sabbath was taken so seriously in some cultures that not doing so was punishable by death. We see remnants of these ancient practices still alive today in our calendars as religions observe portions of Friday, Saturday or Sunday as the sabbath and days of rest.

Today sabbaticals are more commonly known as a year away from work granted every seven years for some professors to step away from the day to day of their normal life and dive into a project, travel, research and/or write a book. Even if you're not a professor, it's understood that if you take a sabbatical, it's a period of time to step away from a productive work mode and get into a more reflective mode, an extended time to rest.

Rest and rejuvenation are vital components in the rhythm of life, yet the boundaries that created pockets of time for it in the past, such as weekends and after business hours, have eroded with advances in technology. Having tiny supercomputers in our hands and the internet at our fingertips can lead us to believe the world is ours to command, but often we're simply becoming more practiced at reacting to what's flowing downstream. The desire for others to connect with us reaches through our phones and into the private spaces formerly reserved for our thoughts alone. We've acclimated ourselves to a new level of 'normal' as we check email from our bedroom pillows, return text messages from the bathroom and listen to podcasts on long walks. The rhythm of life has become so crowded in favor of hyper-connectedness it's as if there are no spaces in between the notes, no time for a rest, to stand back and reflect or listen to that voice inside of us. The natural way of being, living life with built in moments to pause and reflect, has become a luxury in our lives. The responsibility for taking time away from daily demands becomes ours alone. While it seems obvious that rest and self-care are simply part of the natural rhythm in life to be included in our regular schedule, it can be incredibly difficult and nearly impossible to escape the constant connectivity and stimulation of modern life. We've become so focused on what needs to be accomplished, what's happening around us, and what we should respond to that finding the energy to lift ourselves out of the swiftly moving digital current and up onto the shore for a few moments of peace and rest is the furthest thing from our mind.

We need breaks, times of rest when we can bring balance back to our lives. Rest and rejuvenation allow us to make good decisions and be present with those we love. When we step outside of our normal routine, we are presented with an opportunity to reconnect with what's important and alive within us, and reflect on where we are in life. We then return to our normal routine with fresh eyes and a renewed spirit. If we pay attention to the signals that our body sends us, we can better navigate the choices of life; stay focused on the tasks that are important; and cultivate connection, creativity, joy and ease. By taking the time and space to be free, whether a 15-minute coffee break or a weeklong vacation, we become alive to our surroundings, our senses, our dreams. During periods of rest, hearing the voice of our soul – the whisper of ideas, inspiration, and curiosity – gets easier.

WHAT KEEPS Women FROM DOING IT?

Why do women in particular find this such a challenging concept to incorporate into daily life? Many of us simply didn't have it modeled for us as children by our own mothers, so we don't have those subconscious recordings handy to call upon later in life. We grew up in a culture that valued women who sacrificed themselves for the good of the whole more than women who knew their worth and were empowered to use that energy to fuel themselves and everyone around them. We were woven into a fractured fairy tale and learned to play the role of the 'perfect' daughter, friend, leader, partner, mother who gives selflessly and is able to accomplish everything without having any needs of her own. The cultural definition of 'perfect' shifts and changes depending on who is defining it and by its very nature, the goal of perfection is never attainable. Rather than questioning the assumptions at play here, the cultural expectations, or the validity of the fairy tale of perfection, women end up exhausted and believing that the reason they can't live up to these standards is that something's wrong with them, that they're just not enough.

One might expect that as a culture, we're evolving beyond such outdated stereotypes, but in a 2006 study sponsored by Girls, Inc.

74% of girls said they are under pressure to please everyone, up from 60% in 2000.

"It's very difficult because there is so much pressure to be perfect. The media puts pressure on us to be thin, parents put pressure on us to get good grades. We are supposed to be nice. . . . Sometimes it seems unbearable. We just want acceptance."

8TH GRADE GIRL

The way that girls and boys are treated differently in our culture perpetuates this quandary. For example, Caroline Heldman, Associate Professor of Politics at Occidental College, suggests in her TEDx Youth talk that the way we raise our girls harms them. *"We raise our little boys to view their bodies as tools to master their environments. We raise our little girls to view their bodies as projects to constantly be improved."*

If girls grow up to be women who view their bodies as projects to be constantly improved, then is there any end to the quest for improvement? Women are emotionally tangled in their drive to be good "enough", intelligent enough or (whatever the expectation) enough. Constant improvement implies constant movement and a never ending striving for something that can never be obtained. In a recent marketing research project sponsored by Sanctuary Spa, 80% of the women surveyed don't feel "good enough," 40% say they are about to burnout and 72% report that they are their own biggest source of pressure. Unfortunately, there doesn't appear to be a break in sight for them. In 2010, the Gallup-Healthways Wellbeing Index showed that women ages 45 to 64 had the lowest well-being of any age group or gender in America. A woman in this age range fits the profile of the "most stressed out" person in America and medical experts say that this could be the first generation of women who do not outlive their male counterparts by 5-7 years.

"It's the constant feeling that you're never doing enough for any particular group that needs your time. Most definitely, I think that comes with the female territory. I want to find a corner and curl myself up and get away from everybody and everything, but that doesn't happen."

DEBBIE WATKINS,
MIDDLE AGED WOMAN IN U.S.A.

This silent epidemic has women putting pressure on themselves to live up to the unattainable, fictitious status of 'perfect'- destroying their health and well-being - literally taking years off their lives in the process.

I speak from experience, having neglected my inner voice in the past in favor of tuning into the harsh spin cycle demands of a corporate environment. I juggled young children, wishful Martha Stewart-esque attempts at home life, college courses, a failing marriage and operations of a 24/7 helpdesk with the world's largest retailer breathing down my neck. Between self imposed expectations and external demands for my focus and attention, it was all that I could do to jump on the hamster wheel each morning and off again briefly each night. I knew that I was here to make big things happen and I was eager to earn proof from others of my value. I know that the clients I work with today face similar internal challenges feeling so much potential and investing so much energy, yet feeling dissatisfied and unfulfilled with their results regardless of how much they've accomplished. When successful women like Sheryl Sandberg, COO of Facebook and author of *Lean In*, pivot their position on women doing more and admit *"Before, I did not quite get it. I did not really get how hard it is to succeed at work when you are overwhelmed at home,"* you know the source of the problem is beyond any one of us.

Even so, there's an incredibly bright side to this weighty, seemingly impossible scenario. If we are our own biggest source of pressure, this also means we have the power in our hands to give ourselves that massive break we so desperately need, no external permission required. Sure, we were influenced by this mindset of perfectionism, but now that we're aware of it we have the power to choose something different - to control the thoughts in our mind and regain sovereignty in our lives. We can choose to disengage our focus on what is 'wrong' and start training to see what is 'right' about ourselves. Choosing to invest less of our time in the mode of "doing" and more of our time appreciating our state of "being", we let go of the external measures of success and tune in deeply to what is true for us. This allows us to start navigating through life in a way that aligns with who we are, rather than adjusting to meet other's expectations. Guided by our inner authority with direct access to higher levels of enthusiasm and joy, we have the opportunity to live life on our own terms. We can choose to build in regular breaks, to participate in experiences that nourish our heart and soul, and let go of the things that don't serve us. We can give up great things to open ourselves up to that which is even greater.

But how do you actually take a break? A true, restful, don't do anything except for BE kind of extended break?

If you'd asked me that eighteen years ago, I wouldn't have had an answer. I couldn't find time for a break in any moment of any day, let alone an extended rest. There were too many people counting on me, too many responsibilities. And honestly, I was scared of what would happen if I stopped doing so much. Part of me didn't want to pause long enough to take a look at myself and my life. It was easier to keep a slight distance from the truth I knew existed under all the layers of busy, almost as if I were living in a form of suspended reality. Maybe if I ignored it, the discomfort would go away or work itself out. I wouldn't have liked what I found if I faced it head on, it wouldn't have been "enough" for my standards and I wouldn't have known what the hell to do with it.

Today, breaks come easier for me. I know myself better and schedule chunks of time to rest into my calendar. I don't have to run away from my life, I'm happy to be present in most moments and I've ditched most of the guilt. I even welcome kindness and assistance when it's offered (usually). Sometimes I even seek it out. At the time of this writing, receiving is my growth edge.

It's easy to want to put a person writing a book on a pedestal. Don't do that with me. I'm a real person right there with you in the trenches and on the mountain tops. I'm a constant student and guide when it comes to everything in this book. Giving yourself a rest, prioritizing yourself and your down time, and embracing your power and value are major themes I've struggled with my entire life. You could say my life has been and continues to be a training ground for this material. I wouldn't have chosen to be the poster girl for this - it's not so glamorous - but I wouldn't trade it in for anything. When the women I assist see new options for themselves and I get to see their aha's and the return of a spark in their eyes, I know my struggles down this path have a purpose.

As for you and I, together we can make this experience lighter and more fun, and perhaps model a more humane way of walking in this world as empowered, receptive, valued women.

CHAPTER 1
A Primitive Sabbatical

---

*"Opportunities to find deeper
powers within ourselves come when
life seems most challenging."*

JOSEPH CAMPBELL

It wouldn't be fair of me to ask you to go through this process without sharing with you my own, messiness and all. And yet, or of course, this is the part of the book I most resisted writing. Likely because, just like you perhaps, I have a deep and persistent fear of being judged. I suspect it's an aspect of the survival intelligence inherited from my ancestors that tells me it's safer to be accepted and included, rather than be excluded from the tribe. You might not be able to relate directly to the circumstances I'm going to share with you, but I'm certain you'll find a connection in our shared humanity. My version of this journey will look different from yours and so will every other woman's, but we all share this knowing that more is possible, this desire to experience a more congruent life in deeper connection with our divinity.

And so, with my fear of judgement sitting on one shoulder and my deep desire to serve on the other, here is my story...

Eighteen years ago I was your average professionally minded woman: raising a family, working full-time, making myself available for business trips and anything else the 24x7 helpdesk I managed needed from me. Much of my time was devoted to work or day to day family life. In the moments outside of that, we visited family for holidays and to celebrate birthdays. Anytime not spoken for was used to try to get ahead in some way: taking educational classes and studying to improve my ability as a leader at work, figuring out how to best budget and plan for our future, doing home improvements to sell our starter house and move to a better neighborhood or anything else I could think of to catch up to everyone else. My life was full, packed. I was busy. Every moment of every day. And what I know now is that I was attempting to outrun the truth. I was afraid to stop, because I wasn't sure I'd like coming face to face with where I was. Rather than take a rest, I kept pushing, kept *sleepwalking*~~*running*~~ through my perfectly dysfunctional life.

But once I heard the words, "I'm not happy anymore," come out of my then husband's mouth everything came to a halt. I understood the subtext of what he meant and all of the emotions I'd been trying to outrun collided within me. I was overwhelmed with sadness, disappointment, anger, betrayal and it all rushed in during a split second and brought me to the floor. Those soulful whispers I'd been pushing aside now had my full attention. As I sifted through the rubble of my life I could finally see the evidence that had been there all along, the signs that a course correction was needed. Perhaps most shocking was the sudden awareness that I was not the worthless human being I saw reflected back to me in the eyes of the man I was living my life with.

What followed was the hardest, most challenging and gut wrenching days, months and years of my life. I remember... sitting both our kids down on a bench to explain how things would be changing for our family and while our daughter who was 7 seemed to be fine with it, our son who was 3 (and could feel what was happening much more than he could understand the words) burst into tears... my own uncontrollable tears as I watched their father buckle them in for their first outing without me... trying my hardest to focus as I moved my office in for my first day at the new work-at-home job, meanwhile he was moving his things out of our home... For a while we held onto the idea that everything may work out in the end. We tried. But the idea of us staying together was always better than the reality of how we were together. Finally, the clarity came and we accepted that we weren't going to make it, only to discover a couple weeks later that our third child would arrive a month before the divorce would be final.

The intensity only increased as the reality of being a single parent set in and my ex moved out of state. As he was exploring what life was like without the daily responsibility of family, I felt the full weight of all of our choices. The bills - both his and mine - were left for me to pay. The pregnancy was entirely my responsibility, although he did show up the day our son was born and stayed to help that evening. Taking the kids to grief counseling? Me again. Day in and day out the shopping for food, meal prep, cleanup, laundry, diapers, baths and bedtime, breastfeeding, breakfast, driving to and from school, working full-time, pumping breastmilk, handling school parent teacher meetings and events, keeping in touch with family, taxes, being the referee in sibling fights and protecting the youngest from his jealous older brother. The list of responsibilities was endless. Even when I was asleep, I was always "on". If someone stirred, they were mine to comfort.

Having spent so much of my time either working or being with my kids, I hadn't formed friendships in the area since moving from New York years earlier. I felt isolated and alone.

Living in a progressive pocket of the bible belt, I had learned to reveal only as much of my spiritual views as necessary so as to prevent a backlash of judgement and exclusion in the community. I was terrified of letting the people I worked with see who I really was or hear my original thoughts for fear that I'd lose my job and ability to provide for my kids. I spent my days at home telecommuting to my job, on conference calls and in front of the computer. I didn't interact with other people face to face except to pick up or drop off kids. On the weekends, I saw people at our local spiritual center and while I felt loved and accepted there, I didn't see those folks outside of that setting. Gratefully, I met one friend whose divorce was final the same week as mine. Through mutual support, we developed the kind of friendship that allowed us to open up to each other and also call on each other when in need.

Deeply valuing authenticity and collaboration, I wanted my kids to have a school that would nurture their own inner authority rather than expect them to adjust and transform themselves to accommodate the needs of the larger educational institution. I worked with a virtual group and then a local one in hopes of creating such an experience for them, but with too many other responsibilities the project never got off the ground. I wanted us to eat healthier food, and would buy fresh vegetables with the intention of preparing good solid dinners, but ended up going through the drive thru far too often as convenience won out over principles. I simplified and edited as much as I could from our lives to keep up with what I thought was essential and offer what might be just the 'right' conditions so that they would have different options and a better life. I was always striving and never resting. I was mimicking the externals of what I thought was working for others, without understanding an elemental foundation of connection both to my own self and by extension to my children and those we loved. I really thought this was a problem that could be solved with effort, but no matter how much I put in, nothing seemed to budge.

There was a lot of inner turmoil as well. The life I was living was incongruent with what I would learn later about myself. Without knowing it, I had been depriving myself of what I needed to thrive. As an introvert in desperate need of spaciousness and quiet alone time to recharge, I was constantly depleted by my daily activities that required so much energy. Even though I was at home a lot, I was never really alone with quality time to just be. There was always a productive component to my activities and someone depending on me. As a highly sensitive person, I picked up on the emotional state of anyone near me and I carried around a feeling of immense responsibility to make things better for whomever I came in contact with but what I really needed was boundaries and contact with nature. In my attempts to manage the constant demands of single motherhood with three children I had stripped our lives down to the bare bones of what we needed to function. Life felt utilitarian. There was no pleasure.

By the time our youngest was two and a half, I felt like I was going to crack.

When the lease was coming up for renewal on our suburban home, I felt a crisis rising to the surface. I was torn between this practical need for me to work full-time to keep everything going and the desire to spend more time with my kids as they were learning and growing. It occurred to me that THIS was my life: rushing, rushing, rushing. 24x7. There was, at a minimum, sixteen more years of this. Years. And while the kids would get older and become more self-reliant, the fact that I was solely responsible for this family of 4 with no break in sight overwhelmed my thoughts most of my waking hours. Why would we create such a situation in which parents would have to choose between providing for their families and being able to enjoy them? Wasn't something more available? Couldn't we do better for our children, for our families? I remember feeling so frustrated with the options I saw before me. If this was the best situation available within the norms of our society, I wasn't impressed.

> *"We need to rethink our public and corporate workforce policies... We need to build a world where families are embraced and supported and loved... We need to understand that it takes a community to raise children and that so many of our single mothers need and deserve a much more supportive community than we give them. We owe it to them and to their children to do better. We must do more as leaders, as co workers, as neighbors, and as friends."*

SHERYL SANDBERG

I had heard about a teacher up North who would bring his family to our state for the summer. They would live on the lake, unplugged for the season - reading, fishing, camping and enjoying each other. I wanted something like that for me and my kids, some way to take a vacation, to get a break from the daily grind, to step off the hamster wheel of expectations and tune in to see what was real for me and us.

The prospect of renewing the lease on our house felt like it would be giving up and surrendering to the idea that this was just the way things were, that life couldn't be expected to get any better than this, and that my desire for us to live more joyfully was incompatible with our circumstances. The logical choice would have been to renew the lease and continue with the stability of living there, hoping that things would get better with time. But I just couldn't bring myself to do it. Even the architecture, the stark utilitarian aesthetics of the house, mirrored how I felt about our life there. I didn't have an easy alternative, but I could no longer accept this as our only option. My heart yearned for more, to be surrounded by nature and beauty, to feel alive, to be inspired and not settle for less. In a flash of brilliance, a friend who was helping me ponder possibilities offered to let us camp on property she owned in the country in exchange for some work hours each month. My heart could not refuse, it was an enormous, "Yes!"

This opportunity to let go of what we knew, what seemed like the best society had to offer us and to embrace the possibility of something different was exactly what needed to happen at that point. In an extreme move, not one I'd recommend everyone take, we gave notice and started our move into our tent. Our belongings and furniture were either out on the lawn for sale or tucked away inside a storage bin we rented. We kept what was needed for us to live there as well as for me to telecommute from our little piece of country paradise. We moved the trampoline, tent, and refrigerator to the campsite. A friend came and climbed high into the trees to string the 50' x 50' tarp that would become our outdoor living area. I had DSL and electricity turned on at the pole near the dirt road and ran the longest internet cable and extension cords I could buy to the campsite so that I could work and we could power the basics. It was odd, it was clunky, but it made our adventure possible. My heart breathed a sigh of relief being surrounded by so many trees, being so close to the sunshine and breathing fresh air as I worked and went about daily life.

Few understood my choice, let alone supported it. From the outside looking in, it appeared crazy. Later, I even heard that someone considered calling the Department of Human Services to report me for child neglect since we had no running water. Regardless of what anyone else thought, we experienced a summer that will stay with us forever. Mornings waking up to the sunrise, our sleeping bags covered with dew after a night of sleeping under the stars on the trampoline. The whirl and giggles of my daughter and older son getting wound up and then spinning themselves loose on the swing. Jumping on the trampoline until we were silly. Thunderstorms, lightening and playing in the occasional rain. Filling up our large storage containers with water for baths. Reading a book to the kids in which the main character was an owl and then spotting one watching us. Of course there were less glamorous things like going to the bathroom outdoors and potty training the youngest. We never built campfires or used much lighting after dark because I didn't want to draw attention or have people realize we were living there. It was hard enough to explain what we were doing to family and friends, let alone strangers. I'm not sure that I completely understood it myself. For the most part, we would go to sleep when the sun went down and wake up when the sun came up. We returned to our natural rhythms, shared an adventure and reconnected as a family.

The tent summer was hands down the best decision I've ever made in my life. The memories and clarity I gained that summer are priceless and formed the foundation of my commitment to follow those inner nudges, even and especially if they run against the grain of the modern world.

By the time we ended the summer and moved on to our next adventure, the kids seemed much happier and I felt rejuvenated. I cared less about what people thought. I had reconnected to my inner knowing and felt confident again making choices that were in alignment with who I was and what I wanted. I felt more present as a parent and better able to balance the responsibilities of being there for my kids with work. Most of all it was a symbolic middle finger to all of the expectations I had adopted from our culture. It was me

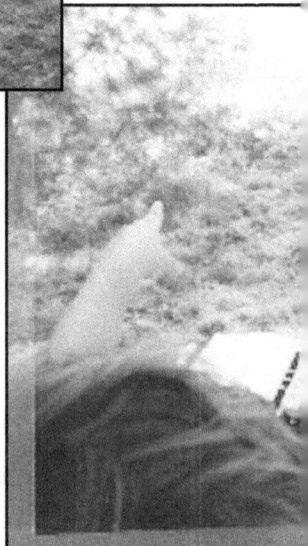

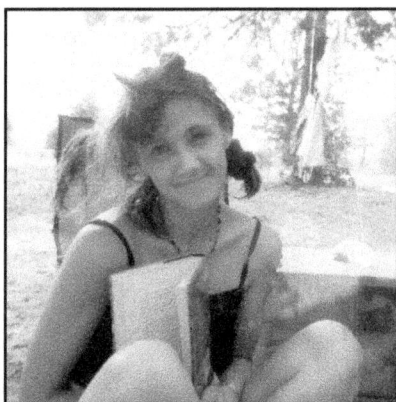

showing the world that what I needed really did matter. I had finally made it onto my own priority list and regardless of what anyone else thought of my choice, I still met all of my responsibilities and the world didn't come crashing down as a result. In fact, I, and the world around me, felt reassembled because of it.

When I asked my middle son what he took away from our summer in the tent, he said, *"learning that you really don't need to have a lot of things or stuff to be happy."* This experience and the value of adventure has stayed with him. At 21, he's already had an urban adventure longboarding and camping along the Pacific coast; gone on extended trips to Virginia, Washington and Oregon; and walked across the state of Arkansas solo, camping along the way. Recently, he called me using Facetime to say "Hi," and asked me to guess where he was. He flipped the view so that I could see he was standing at the edge of the Grand Canyon. He's spiritually grounded, has a compassionate heart, and takes my breath away each time I see him do his next big thing. He is my proof that including my need for rest among the litany of priorities was a good decision. Life *can* be whatever we choose.

But I don't claim to have it all figured out. I'm not sure any of us ever do. Ultimately, we're just making it up as we go along and doing the best we can with the awareness and resources we have at the time. I consider myself a constant student of life and within the Human Design typing system, I'm an Investigative Martyr. I am life's crash test person. I strap in and do life experiments, often those that others won't do, to find out what works and what doesn't. Then I come back and share my findings so that you can know what routes hold no promise and which ones contain a gold mine.

I can tell you now that sticking with the mindset of self-sacrifice doesn't serve you or your family in the way you think it will. My life changed only when I finally chose to create room for myself and my own needs in my busy life. I chose to be valuable and to respond to the inner nudges of my soul that were calling for solitude, connection with nature and a rest from what had been our norm. That's where I found the gold mine.

If you're frustrated with life, you don't have to live by default and you don't have to sacrifice any part of you for someone else to have what they want. There's nothing fruitful down that road for you, nor for humanity. Regardless of what we've been conditioned to think with stories, movies, religions and cultural norms, you are inherently worthy. You simply being here matters and you don't need to exhaust yourself in an effort to prove your value. We don't make the world better when we give up who we are for others. That might have been useful for survival in the past when resources were scarce and life was dangerous, but now we can live our day to day with much more ease. What is most required of us today is to truly show up for ourselves, fully and completely, holding nothing back.

In fact, I think this is one thing those of us who have the habit of self-sacrifice got wrong. In an effort to create more space for others, we collapsed our needs, wants and desires but what if breathing life into our needs, wants and desires is exactly what this world needs? I have this hunch that when more of us who've been holding aspects of ourselves back become willing to stand up and live the life we dare to dream, we will end up sharing the love and compassion we find for ourselves with everyone we meet. I see this as one of the ways we create a more loving and compassionate world for our children and grandchildren. We must start with ourselves. As Ghandi said, being the change we wish to see. Rather than resisting, I think the world will gratefully receive us.

Now I promise that you don't have to do something drastic during your sabbatical like move out of your home and live in a tent (unless you want to). What you will find in the pages that lay ahead is the opportunity to make adjustments that are tailored and meaningful to you and where you are in your life right now. You'll be able to connect directly with your inner wisdom and navigate whatever challenges or opportunities come your way.

So I would love to claim that after our summer in the tent I never again found myself overwhelmed by life and was happily living each day with self-care as my first priority, but that wasn't the case. The summer in the tent had given me a deep reconnection to myself and my values but in such an extreme situation that was hard to replicate once we got back to "normal" life. Almost a decade later I once again found myself exhausted and depleted from serving others, overcommitting, always saying "yes" to the requests people made of me...

CHAPTER 2
A Modern Sabbatical

"No one else can define your truth for you, you have to define it for yourself."

NILOFER MERCHANT

As life evolved beyond that summer in the tent we moved to a cozy little village in the Ozark hills. While I had been born in a small town, my family moved away from it early in elementary school and my memories and experiences came from living in more populated areas like Oklahoma City, San Diego, and Manhattan, before planting roots in Northwest Arkansas. For years, I had harbored a romantic notion of what it must be like to live in this tiny little village with brightly painted houses tucked into the hills, several Bed & Breakfasts on each corner, the buildings filled with galleries, artists and creatives at every turn. The community is powered by two divergent philosophical viewpoints, the woo woo creatives and strictly religious, and yet somehow they coexist peacefully as various festivals and conventions reflecting each viewpoint invade and swell the occupancy during summer weekends. Gay Pride and Diversity weekend bring thousands of people and a surge of revenue with people traveling in to see the Great Passion Play presented each night. Overlooking the events stands one of the largest statues of Christ, pleased I'm sure at how well everyone is getting along.

We also found here an alternative school, up and running since the 70's. I had determined that our experiment with homeschooling and unschooling wasn't sustainable while telecommuting to my full time job so this new option gave my children the values and learning structure I knew would suit them better than the public system. Settling in this town, I felt the essence of being cradled in a mother's arms, safe, accepted, and the perfect place to land after our summer adventure.

Fast forward through the next nine years and you'd see that I'd regained the ability to feel more deeply, cultivate the skills to be more aware of my desires and learn by trial and error through the practice of incorporating more of what I love in life. Each choice presented an opportunity to stop living by default and start aligning with what was true and nurturing for me. As I experimented with choosing what was in alignment with my true nature, rather than what was expected or assumed, I experienced the magic and energy that must have always been available to me but had lain hidden. I began to relax into a deeper connection with myself and felt less resistance in life as the choices I made supported both my needs and values.

From the choice to move back to a more populated area, to buying a house without being able to see inside of it as it was auctioned off at the courthouse steps, to leaving my well paying corporate job to learn about running a small business - each step called me closer to alignment, closer to arranging life to suit me and my kids rather than having us change who we are to fit in with what was available. These weren't easy or fearless choices, they were filled with risk, tension and uncertainty, but they were what my heart was calling for and I was learning to heed that call and to trust it.

The kids were growing, life still had challenges and not everything was magical, but overall I felt more energy than I could remember having since I was a kid. I channeled it all outward into the new possibilities I saw before me. I met my current husband and we started a new life together in a home we thought would be the perfect launching pad for our dreams. I started taking steps to fulfill on that promise to give back to women who felt stuck like I did and I was investing all of my time, energy and resources in projects and people I loved.

Rationally everything looked good on the outside, but on the inside I was cratering again. This time, rather than to the responsibility that I felt I inherited or to the expectations I felt from the outside world,

I was cratering under commitments and responsibilities I had freely and consciously chosen to be involved with and commit to. They were all things I loved and felt passionate about. They were things that I knew would make a difference in the world, they were worthy of my time and attention, yet I found myself in a similar state of overwhelm. This time, overwhelmed by a lot of really awesome things that taken individually would make sense to participate in, but collectively created a huge outpouring of time and energy. Rather than energizing me, the collective weight was draining me.

I was face to face with an unexpected dilemma. There's so much out there about following your passions and pursuing projects that feed your soul, but there's a caveat that's not always discussed. The saying that 'women can have it all' is misleading. We have so many options available to us, yet we've been conditioned to channel our energy in care and service of others with little understanding for how to make sure that we have something at the end of the day for ourselves. Without the skill of evaluating trade-offs and including ourselves as a priority in life - knowing we are inherently worthy regardless of what we can 'do' for others - we run the risk of continual burnout even from the things we love most.

There's a fine balance to modern life and I was learning on the front lines how vital it is to have boundaries, to be able to say 'no' (even to things that you're passionate about) so that you can have time for yourself too. It's not as simple as having it all and while I had learned how to connect with my inner wisdom and discern what my heart was calling for, I was just beginning to understand how to navigate a complex world of possibilities with myself as my constant in a sea of variables.

To give you an idea of what my life looked like, I considered these my primary roles:

- Mother of two kids at home, one out of the house, doing all that being a parent entails (taxi driver, chef, counselor, tutor, mediator, personal shopper, provider, accountant, etc.)

- President of the board for a local spiritual center during a time of transition and crisis

- Logistics Coordinator at a large corporation working 40-60 hours a week

- Teacher of youth spiritual lessons once a month

- Participant of environmental sustainability group at the spiritual center, the local faith alliance sustainability group and a citizen-based green economy group.

- Participant of the communications team at the spiritual center

- Owner of a side business requiring weekly and monthly chunks of focused time

- Co-Founder and participant in weekly mastermind group

- Landlord of my first rental house, which turns out can be demanding at the most inconvenient times

- Partner to an amazing man who, as you can guess, didn't see me much outside of the groups we participated in together

- And all around competent 'yes' gal for nearly every additional request that came to me

My schedule was packed to the minute. I was there and I was willing. I wanted to serve and make a positive difference in the world, but even though I was surrounded by opportunities that aligned beautifully with my values, I neglected to factor in my own personal time. I look back and wonder 'WHAT was I thinking?!' To tell the truth, I wasn't.

Despite everything I had learned and experienced, I had fallen back into a rut of living from the outside in; reacting and responding to everyone and everything around me, and operating from external priorities rather than living an aligned life from the inside out.

I wasn't even showing up at the end of my own priority list. What makes this worse is that at the same time, I was working on that commitment I had made so many years ago and creating the building blocks of THIS very program you are participating in (go ahead, you can chuckle at the irony, I'm grinning as I type this). I had come so far from where I started, only to find myself not being able to recognize the water I was swimming in for what it was. Thankfully, I had the wise counsel of my fabulous coach, DJ Sie, who helped me get straight. Making lemonade of my experience, I leveraged what I had learned into the next evolution of a sabbatical that more closely resembles the *Sabbatical from "Yes"* as outlined in this book.

Once I made the decision to take a sabbatical, my time freed up. I gained clarity about what commitments were fueling me more than others and which ones were requiring more of my energy. I resigned from the board position and let go of the teaching and committee positions. And no, when I stopped doing those things, the world didn't end. I kept the responsibilities that added more energy to my life such as parenting, my relationship with my partner, the master minding group and working on my side business.

Instead of spending so many hours each week contributing in those other roles, I was able to do things I had rarely made time for before, such as taking myself on mini-retreats, creating art, walking in the woods and even just sitting in a comfortable chair and BEing. No agenda, nobody to see me, approve of me, or evaluate me, but me.

I view this period as being similar to someone healing from post-traumatic stress. I just needed time and space to simply BE.

When I was asked if I could help or do something for someone, I would decline saying that I was focusing on self-care. Believe me, it was challenging to sit on my hands and NOT volunteer because that had been my learned reaction to requests. For most of my life, my self-identity had been wrapped up in what I could do for others. I admit that I was paranoid because I now seemed invisible. In the past, people could always rely on me for help but now they couldn't so I just seemed to fade into the background. That took a little getting used to, but it was required for me to be seen for ME, rather than for what I did for others.

My worth shifted from being dependent on me doing things for others to me being worthy all the time, no matter what, simply because I exist.

Once I finally started putting myself first again, I returned to making decisions from a place of internal alignment. This time, I was more keenly aware that even in a life with an abundance of things I love, there is always a priority list and I need to be at the top of it. I included more things that were nurturing and energizing and my life took off in an even more positive direction and for THAT, I am eternally grateful. It was incredible how things in my external life also lined up and seemed to work out with less effort. Now, when I look back, it's hard to believe that person was me. I think differently, I carry myself differently, I respond differently and I evaluate requests differently. I'm more ME now and NOT the person I think others want or need me to be.

Living in our modern, hyper-connected world as a woman comes with so many opportunities, opinions and pulls for your time yet when you're anchored into what's true for you, you can navigate all the complexities with more joy and less stress. As you consider what this might look like in your own life, you might be worried about disappointing all of the people you have been accustomed to pleasing in the past. If so I can tell you that in most cases the people who resist your changes will either learn to adjust to your new expectations - possibly even respecting you and themselves more for it - or they will fall away out of your life. This can be a scary proposition, but trust me, you want people by your side who value, appreciate and love you for who you really are, not for what you can do for them.

Your authentic self is far more valuable than you can imagine, not only for yourself, but for those around you and the rest of the world.

My role in this journey is to be your guide and lead you through this experiment with compassion, curiosity and love. There is a term used by the Institute for Integrative Nutrition called *bio-individuality*. It refers to the fact that regardless of all of the research, expert programs and opinions about diet and nutrition, there is no single diet or nutritional program that is right for everyone. We are not clones. We are unique and biologically diverse beings with unique sets of environmental conditions, genetic coding and emotional make-ups. As such, bio-individuality suggests that there are many beneficial diets that can be considered the 'right' one, possibly as many as there are humans. One person's food can be another person's poison. Each individual can only figure out what's best for them by taking personal responsibility, tuning into their body and observing their reactions. And this can change over time. What worked for you in your twenties will likely change in your thirties, forties and beyond. You have to be continually present in your own life and pay attention in order to find the wellness you seek.

The aspects of the *Self-Full Living Framework* you'll find in this book extend the concept of bio-individuality into every aspect of your life. With this book, you have a container for an experience within which you can determine your own unique life situation - the one that is best suited for you with the most optimal conditions for who you are. This won't happen overnight, nor will it be completed in 30 days, but you'll have a foundation in place to support you in finding what works for you from this point forward.

In the coming chapters I'll ask you questions as well as offer you opportunities to see things differently than you might have in the past, all of which is designed to lead you to a deeper, stronger, more clear connection with yourself. This book will hold your sacred intentions and confidential conversations with yourself, providing a container for your experience with an open, playful and sometimes indirect approach to challenging assumptions that appear to keep you stuck. Then as you determine what changes you would like to make, I'll help you step into *Self-Full Living*, mining those precious nuggets of wisdom found along the way so that you can make choices about how you want to invest them for your future. Throughout this book, I am here to be an advocate for you and your highest version of yourself. This is my passion and an honor.

CHAPTER 3
Centering

"The hardest thing to learn is self-love. If you do not infuse yourself with love, how can you awaken it in others? Self-love takes practice. Self-love comes from living in ways that do not betray your integrity. It comes by living your truth. One must be meticulously honest with ourselves. It is in the little self-delusions where we tend to avoid looking at our own lower self's intent or actions that betray our integrity and decrease our healing power. Your integrity and wholeness affect all sentient beings upon the face of the earth; indeed the earth itself."

BARBARA BRENNAN

And so we begin...

Allow me to take a moment to say "Welcome" and "I'm so glad you're here." It's one thing to share my story with you and an entirely different experience for you to experiment with it in the laboratory of your own life. If your heart is calling you to this, and I'm guessing it is because we're still meeting here inside these pages, know that there's something here for you to discover about yourself, about life. Please consider this your invitation to come inside, take a look around and see what's involved before making the commitment to explore it for yourself.

If you haven't already suspected it, you'll soon see how this is a process that cannot be outsourced to someone else. Jim Rohn said, *"You can't hire someone else to do your push-ups for you,"* and it's the same here, you can't outsource self-care, self-respect or self-love. If you want the results, you've got to be willing to make it happen. Most of the time, when women find me they've been hit with a challenge that could be perceived as a 'hammer' in their lives. It might be that a relationship they've invested so much of themselves in breaks-up and they realize they have little left for themselves... or a health crisis that puts them face to face with their mortality... or a sense of complete overwhelm and a realization that they've been running on energy fumes that are about to run out. Some might have powered through positive experiences that they wanted such as grad school, only to find that they somehow lost touch with their dreams and desires in the process. These situations are opportunities to be leveraged as they break through the barriers of protection we've accumulated and present us with situations that feel as if they will break us open and rip us apart. In a sense, that is exactly what's happening. But it's not to break our will, it's to reveal our true essence. It could be viewed as a demolition process to break down what no longer serves us so that we can rebuild on a solid foundation in a way that is nourishing and nurturing to our authenticity. Life can then serve us, rather than us serving life.

So here's what I know about you...

Chances are you're a compassionate, sensitive, driven woman who feels pulled to the natural world. You're highly intelligent and can feel there's a lot of potential inside you wanting to come out. You can sense when something is off in a room or for a person, your bullshit detector works extremely well. You're probably more spiritual than religious and you're curious about a lot of things. From the outside looking in, your life looks pretty pulled together, but on the inside something's missing. You're feeling disconnected from your core, from your dreams and your desires. You find yourself knowing what you 'should' do to care for yourself, but mustering up the attempts to get it done is hard and when you make it to happen, it is only temporary, rather than habit.

You're also incredibly self-reliant, maybe you're even known as the "responsible one." When faced with a crisis or a problem, you push through it, even if that means putting yourself aside and others first to keep things afloat. People can count on you to be there, to be a good listener and to care, even at the expense of your own schedule and well-being.

If this sounds like you, I mean this in the most loving way... Stop being so damn competent! Please hear me and really take this to heart...

Give yourself a rest from being the primary person who does everything, who feels responsible and tries to make things happen all on her own.

Give yourself the experience of opening up to allow new tools, options and support to show up.

Give yourself time to experiment making change in the company of others.

Give yourself permission to lean on others and experience the value of being vulnerable, of asking for what you want, of allowing a trusted person to share in your inner thoughts, fears, insecurities and feelings.

Let yourself experiment, get messy and risk doing it all wrong. Accept the possibility that you could choose to let go of some of your responsibilities, turning them over to another capable soul or just giving them up... and see what happens. Open yourself to the experience of not being the go-to person. Let yourself relax with no agenda, nothing to do.

You might find this a scary proposition if you're incredibly self-reliant, value being productive and find having control comforting. It can be challenging to let go of the predictability we try to create with these modes of operating and venture into the realm of uncertainty. But by risking vulnerability, letting people see our imperfections and embracing the unknown through our interaction with others, we are moving beyond the survival tactics that got us to this (stuck) point in life. It is these survival tactics that keep us from reaching higher levels of thriving. The very tendency to be so damned independent and competent is the very thing that holds you back from receiving the perspective, insights and assistance that will catapult you to an entirely new level of creativity and freedom. Nevermind that nagging thought in the back of your mind about taking up too much time or another person's attention. That's just your scales of balance, which are inaccurately calibrated to have you carrying far more than your fair share of responsibility.

Intellectually, we understand that taking time for ourselves as a human being is not a crime, nor an offense. But the guilt we feel isn't rational, it's emotional. We're under the influence of a three shot cocktail: the perfectionism to do it well, the pressure to do it all and the belief it should be done for others. It's shelf life doesn't expire as it's preserved by the tendency for women to internalize the failure to meet these expectations as a reflection of her intelligence or value. A recent survey done by *Stylist Magazine* found that 96% of women feel guilty at least once a day. For almost half, its up to four times a day. The most attributed reasons for feeling guilty were eating unhealthily followed by not spending enough time with family or on work.

Even a logical attempt to challenge this guilt is entangled with emotion, but it's important that we understand why our viewpoint as women matters and why stepping into our power, feeling energized and showing up fully can benefit the world. There's a fundamental difference between the female and male brain. *"The female brain is predominantly hardwired for empathy. The male brain is predominantly hardwired for understanding and building systems,"* writes Cambridge University neuroscientist, Simon Baron-Cohen in his book, *The Essential Difference.*

You could say women are the connective tissue of humanity. Language and fine motor skills develop about six years earlier in girls than in boys. As we grow into women, our brains have more white matter than men, which means more connection between the left and right hemispheres. This holistic thinking along with our ability to more accurately identify emotions gives us an advantage in accessing language skills to build relationships - we naturally see the connections and make choices that will benefit the whole. The trick for us is to not get lost in the whole, pushing our own needs aside in an attempt to do what is best for others.

For example, United States Senator Kirsten Gillibrand recognizes the positive effect of women showing up in government, *"We bring a different lens to problem-solving, and that balancing perspective often leads to better results. I have seen for myself that when women are at the table, a broader agenda is discussed – an agenda that looks out for all Americans, particularly those who have no voice."* Suze Orman, author and financial advisor, sees it through the lens of personal finance, *"Men and women both have an equal capacity to make money, but they want money for different reasons. Men want money for power and women want it for comfort, and usually not their own comfort, but the comfort of others in their lives."*

My heart yearns to see more of this, more women's perspectives in all facets of life. But understand an interesting irony here, anything that sacrifices our personal energy and enthusiasm ends up diminishing what is available for the whole. Therefore, investing in exquisite self-care for ourselves ensures that we show up as our most energized and creative selves, it is how we best serve others. It's up to us to shift our perception and truly see ourselves as we are: vital, radiant individuals, uniquely positioned to be able to see our world holistically and recognize connections that would go unnoticed if we neglected to speak up. If you're typically a loner or someone who has built up protective mechanisms so that you can function in the world, then you also stand to gain the most from revealing yourself and standing as an advocate for the greater benefit of all involved. Marianne Williamson's voice echos in my mind at this point, "Your playing small does not serve the world. There is nothing enlightened about shrinking so other people won't feel insecure around you. We are all meant to shine..."

Imagine a world filled with rejuvenated and empowered women, naturally extending our energy to those around us. Investments made in honoring, caring and empowering ourselves having a benefit on our families and communities. Investing in ourselves is a win-win situation. Feeling rejuvenated while seeing how those we love appreciate our full attention and peaceful presence makes us want more of it. In the most simple terms, when we don't take time for ourselves, we're depriving the people we love from progress. How's that for a little guilt reverse psychology?

As an empowered, well rested, aligned woman, I have no doubt that you will spread the love.

Now imagine clusters of empowered women gathering together and learning to be fierce allies and advocates for themselves and one another. Let's set aside the common perspective that we are in constant competition with each other, that's simply a divisive tactic, and embrace the vision of us weaving together a shared vision of connection, support and collaboration that benefits us as individuals as well as the whole. New possibilities for humanity are born and cultivated in the coffee shops, living rooms, and on park benches where small groups of women gather together to talk about their dreams and desires, to hold space for each other, to listen deeply with open hearts and to yield to our collective yearning.

To bridge the geographical distance that stands between us and other women on this path, I've started a virtual meeting space using Facebook. *Live True to You* is a private group I moderate and it's open to any woman who resonates with this work. You can read more about it and how to access it under "Join the Tribe" in the resources listed below. Consider this your personal invitation, I'd love to 'meet' you inside and have a chance to interact with you there.

By sharing your insights, celebrating the aha's and requesting assistance with challenges or brainstorming, you're creating real connection with other women and when witnessing them doing the same, the shifts of perspective and learning occur exponentially. It's as if you're learning and shifting through the eyes and lifetimes of each woman participating, and that creates the conditions for great depths of compassion, humility and respect. We see ourselves through the eyes of another and we know we are not alone, that we don't have to bear the burden of making changes that can feel monumental on our own. We can share the experience and lend our strength, love and wisdom. Together, we can do so much more than we can alone.

Take a moment now to make your journey easier and more fluid by connecting with a loving and supportive community and accessing the multimedia resources available to deepen your experience:

❏ **Gather Your Peeps** - Pull together a friend or two, or even your book study group and take the *Sabbatical from "Yes"* together. It doesn't have to be a large group, but it is ideal if you partner with at least one other person for accountability.

❏ **Join the Tribe** - Join our heart-centered and subtly subversive private Facebook group where we stand together as fierce allies and advocates for ourselves and each other living a life that's true to each of us. This is a place for bright, sensitive, heart-centered women who want to connect with others embracing their personal power. We don't claim to have all the answers and we might be scared shitless, but we're willing to get messy in the process of experimenting, playing with the possibilities and seeing what works. Find us here: **www.christidaniels.com/community**

❏ **Access the Multimedia Resources** - This is so much more than a book! Take the opportunity to integrate this work on a deeper level (especially if your dominant learning style isn't visual) and access all the multimedia resources: Download the companion workbook, listen to audio versions of each exercise, read articles and listen to interviews with women who are learning to prioritize themselves in life... The material is always evolving and you'll be able to access new insights and information as it becomes available. Go here to access this rich learning experience: **www.christidaniels.com/goodies**

Watch for this symbol: ◀))

You'll find the media symbol throughout the
book when additional resources are available.

Approach the chapters that follow as an experiment and an investigation into the unknown. It will be important to bring a sense of curiosity with you and a desire for making discoveries. There is no right or wrong here. No mistakes. Just a lot of observing, pondering, wondering, and discovering. Trust that you're the world's best expert on YOU. This is your journey. I don't have your answers, only you do. You own your experience and I trust that you will bring your most full self to each reading and every exercise. You will experience a shift to the extent that you participate and do the work. The more you put in, the more you'll get out.

If things seem overwhelming, I trust you to make the choices only you can make to take the best possible care of yourself. Despite the value of independence many of us were raised with, asking for assistance is not a sign of weakness nor incompetence. It's a wise and loving thing to do when you're struggling, which happens to everyone, even if it's not something that's discussed widely nor visibly. Reach out to our online community, your local friends, family, and emotional support team, or even a professional should you require additional support. Be committed to the experience you deserve and the support you need to make it happen.

You are worth it.

Now, let's do this!

CHAPTER 4
Preparation

"All of life is an experiment.
The more experiments you make the better."

RALPH WALDO EMERSON

Before you start your sabbatical, there are a few preparation steps that will assist you in seeing how these cultural influences have crept into your own life and what you stand to gain from transcending your zone of familiarity. First, we'll take a look at the broader picture before we narrow our focus to your experience.

Self-sacrifice by women is something I grew up seeing and understanding as a way of life. I know I'm not alone. The feminine is viewed as flexible and fluid, which is an incredible gift; however being able to adjust to whatever comes your way can be detrimental if you aren't showing up as a priority in your own life, especially if all you're doing is bending and contorting to meet everyone else's needs at the expense of your own.

Living life from a place of self-sacrifice robs women of their true lives, potential, happiness, authenticity, intimacy, connection, self-worth, pleasure, desire, dreams, fun, creativity, and genius. It also robs humanity of benefiting from the full presence and contribution of women, half the human race! I think it's a condition that's more serious than any of the diseases and health conditions that have a multitude of drug companies developing cures for them.

This is a silent loss, but one that happens each and every day. The symptoms can be ignored and the situation can be pushed aside, undetected for years and, sadly, even lifetimes. Every day that a woman defers her drive and passion in favor of putting someone else's needs, wants and desires ahead of her own, we have lost her inner spark of aliveness - a most precious resource that could fuel her and everyone around her.

"Before you know it, what ends up happening is the person who's always saying "yes" when they really want to say "no" builds a state of chronic resentment in the body, an energy field, in their lives. That resentment, I believe, is a source of many of the illnesses that we see."

CHERYL RICHARDSON

When we continue to live lives riddled with self-sacrifice, ignoring the vibrant soulful desires inside of us, the next generation watches, unaware that they are being encoded to repeat what they are seeing. And the cycle continues...

"Nothing has a stronger influence psychologically on their environment and especially on their children than the unlived life of the parent."

C.G. JUNG

It is my belief that women collectively hold the key to many of the solutions that our culture desperately needs, the solutions that would infuse a sense of peace, joy and compassion into our politics, negotiations, organizations and society. But unless these women are nurturing and valuing themselves at high levels, tuning into their authenticity and putting themselves in the position of achieving their own divinely inspired dreams, our world will lose out on their presence and their gifts. These women will lose out on the experience of fulfillment in seeing their dreams and potential come to full expression. As Wayne Dyer has said, they might *'die with their music still inside.'*

Elizabeth Gilbert touched on this subject in her book, *Committed*, in which she coined the phrase *"New England Cemetery Syndrome"* to describe this modern condition of deprivation. She writes that if you visit any New England graveyard, you'll find it filled with centuries of clusters of family gravestones that provide insight into the lives of the women who lived during that time. You'll find the infants who died each winter, buried in rows. Think of how challenging and heart wrenching such a woman's life must have been then. Knowing the strength of women, we can assume that they did what they had to and made it through to see the next Spring.

Gilbert points out that as modern women we are lucky to have moved beyond such brutal conditions, but that this doesn't necessarily mean we don't deal with grieving and loss from situations that we are presented with in our own lives. She suggests that many women carry within them an entire cemetery within which they've buried the dreams and desires they gave up for their families, yet have moved on to survive and do what they thought they had to do. She writes that women *"...become selfless to the point of near invisibility in order to construct these exemplary environments for their families..."* She moves on to propose a conversation about how we might collaborate to create a world where *"healthy children can be raised and healthy families can prosper, without women having to scrape bare the walls of their own souls to do it..."*

Her words linger in my mind and cause my belly to feel hollow, like a cavern. I recognize the scarcity thinking and emptiness of living that way in my own life. The conversation that she proposes just happens to be the very one that we're engaging with and expanding within this book and the *Self-Full Living Framework*. Rather than perpetuating a culture of scarcity that expects women to deprive themselves in order for others to have what they desire, you and I are creating an abundant world where women are connected so deeply to themselves, value themselves at such high levels and fill their energy reserves to overflowing so that the grace, energy and presence within them spills over into everyone nearby. I believe that we can create a world that honors and values everyone in it and doesn't require anyone to give up who they are so that others can have what they want.

This is a monumental shift in our culture and I'm so glad you're on board, not only for the benefits to your own life, but the contribution you'll be making to the world at large through being exactly who you are and recognizing and honoring your value. I get excited thinking about the next generation seeing those of us who dare to, walk the path of exquisite self-care and love. The positive effect this will have on their lives is immeasurable and will ripple through all the generations to come. At some point, I'd love to see women outgrow the need for this work, for high self value and honoring of ourselves to become so firmly in place that this work seems archaic and just fades away.

But before that can happen, we need to pull this topic close to us and take a brief look back to reflect on where we've been so that it can inform our focus moving forward. For this to fit easily into your life, you might choose to give yourself several days or one week to complete the preparation steps. By completing one exercise each day, you'll give yourself space for additional insights to show up in between the exercises. This can deepen your resolve and commitment to your own *Sabbatical from "Yes."*

As we begin the steps that will lead you to your sabbatical, you might find yourself feeling a bit resistant to the actual work. Sure, it's interesting to read about my story and the rah-rah-rah "let's make the world a better place" bit, but as if you need another thing to add to your list of to-dos... Oh, sweet sister, I wouldn't ask you to do anything without there being a very big and important end result in it for you. You might not see the change right away, but we're diverting years, in some cases decades, of habits. And you're going to feel a bit strange simply because it's different.

Here's my promise to you: If you do this work and you give it your honest best effort, you are going to see shifts begin to happen. First in your thinking, then your feelings and eventually your choices, which will affect your outcomes. If you were happy with life as it is right now, you wouldn't be reading these words. You know there's something calling you forward and the way for you to move toward it is through these unconventional steps. There's a method to my approach, we're bypassing your logical mind and getting straight to the heart of the matter. So now, let's not give your mind too much time to ponder this, go ahead and jump wholeheartedly into the exercises.

PREPARATION STEP 1:
Initial Questions

🔊))

These first questions are going to prime the pump and get you connected with how this topic has shown up in your life. Pretend this is the deep end of the pool and dive right into them. Be painstakingly honest with yourself here, almost as if you were a journalist reporting on what you've witnessed. And remember to bring a sense of curiosity; you're on an investigation and moving through a process of discovery. Please make sure that you have at least 30 minutes of uninterrupted time to complete them.

What brought you to this book?
(please be specific)

Look back at your answer to the last question, how does your answer as well as expectations of others show up in your life?

Thinking about your previous answers, use the grid below to identify at least 3-5 specific situations in your life where the expectations of others direct your actions and choices.

| SITUATION | RATE | | | | |
	Low				High
	1	2	3	4	5
	1	2	3	4	5
	1	2	3	4	5
	1	2	3	4	5
	1	2	3	4	5

Go back through each situation and rate your level of frustration with it using 1=low and 5=high.

When it comes to what prompted you to read this book and/or the expectations of others, what is your biggest frustration? (Remember to be specific)

When it comes to what prompted you to read this book and/or the expectations of others, what have you tried so far that DID NOT work? (Remember to be specific)

What do you think the solution IS or what would you like it to be?

How would your life be different if you could resolve this situation immediately?

Kudos to you for getting those questions answered! Now, if you're noticing an urge to move forward with the next exercise, I recommend putting this work aside for a day and returning to it tomorrow. If you're noticing the urge to stop now, I recommend you go ahead and continue. You might think these suggestions are odd, given the fact that we're here to tune into our inner wisdom and I'm asking you to do the opposite in this moment. But we're also here to shift the way of being that brought you to this place and it's in that spirit that I ask you to do the opposite of what you may think is best right now.

Now that we're diving into some of the underlying feelings that are fueling you, let's give them a way to play....

Your inner child is an aspect of your inner wisdom. She has a different perspective on you and your life, one that's not always available in daily lives. If she's anything like my inner child, she's had to go underground and live in darkness to preserve her innocence. In this next exercise, we're honoring her wherever she is by opening up the channels of communication through a medium that's familiar to most children, drawing and coloring. By providing this page and offering it up to her so that she can speak, we are gifting her with a spot here at the table to lend us her perspective, to get things off her chest and to offer her unique form of wisdom. We're going to do this by using your non-dominant hand, letting your inner child take control over it and use it to say what she's been longing to say through images and words.

PREPARATION STEP 2:
Wanted Poster

🔊

Let's pretend we're back in a kindergarten classroom for this next exercise... We'll be imagining that there's a **"Putting Others First Villain"** that's been running throughout the country. In order to identify and contain it, we need to know exactly what it looks like and how it's shown up in your own life. Through this, you'll see what putting others first looks like through the eyes of your inner child and what you stand to gain from transcending its effects.

Make sure that you have uninterrupted time to focus on this exercise. You can expect to complete it within 15-20 minutes, but allow yourself 30 so that you're not rushed. Give yourself permission to let go a bit and have fun with this!

To begin, start by gathering something colorful to write with (ie. markers, crayons or colored pencils). Next, sit in a comfortable position and take several deep breaths. Put a hand over your heart and breath into your heart. Recall a time when you felt intense gratitude. Let that feeling expand until it fills your entire body and sit with that feeling for a couple of minutes.

WANTED

(1) The Putting Others First Villian	(2) Has stolen from me...

(3) When I transcend POF, my reward will be...

(4) My new mantra is...

Ask your heart to show you what your strain of the **"Putting Others First Villain"** looks like. Use the hand that you rarely write with, your non-dominant hand, to draw what it looks like in the box labeled **"Putting Others First Villain."** For some, rather than seeing an image in your mind, you might just need to put a crayon, colored pencil or marker in your hand and let it take the lead drawing the picture, before we're sure what it will look like. Whatever way works best for you. It could feel strange and child-like, and that's exactly how it's supposed to feel. Go with it.

Look at your drawing and ask it to tell you what it has stolen from you. Use the hand you rarely write with, your non-dominant hand, to write or draw what comes to mind in the box **"Has Stolen from me."**

Ask your heart to show you what your reward will be for transcending the effects of the **"Putting Others First Villain."** Use the hand you rarely write with, your non-dominant hand, to write or draw what your reward will be in the box **"When I transcend this, my reward will be...."**

This time, switch over to the hand you usually write with, your dominant hand and write a 2-3 word phrase that sums up what your reward will be at the bottom of the poster in the box **"My New Mantra Is."** Circle that phrase in red. You now have your focal point for your *Sabbatical from "Yes."*

I know it can feel strange to allow your inner child to express her perception of what's been taken from you and what you stand to gain. I congratulate you for daring to look her way, for diving into something that feels so different. Your inner child is able to see things you don't have access to with your logical mind, she's much more in touch with your heart and with the aspects of yourself you've likely pushed aside. Those heart-felt aspects are integral to the work we're doing here. You can think of the mantra you identified at the end as an expression of your soul's desire, what your inner wisdom is calling forth through this sabbatical process. Take a moment to earmark this page, you'll want to come back to revisit it.

While we're reflecting on loss and restoration, the story 'La Loba' comes to mind. In the book *Women Who Run with the Wolves*, Dr. Clarissa Pinkola Estes tells of a wild woman whose work is to collect the bones of wolves. She collects the bones to preserve them until they can be reassembled into a complete skeleton and restored again. In order to restore them, she sings over the bones and breathes life into them. The body of a wolf rises up, begins to move, then runs off into the night transforming into the figure of a woman.

The bones in this story represent for me the lost parts of us that were given away, stolen, left behind or buried in the inner cemetery Elizabeth Gilbert wrote about. The next exercise is an opportunity for you to take a survey of the headstones that might be found in your own inner cemetery and make a conscious choice to collect some of the bones needed in order to create the structure of the new version of yourself that is ready to rise up.

As an example of this process I'll share a time in my life when I walked through something similar. My amazing coach, DJ Sie, encouraged me to get away so that I could get in touch with myself during a time when I felt creatively blocked. I went off into the woods for a day long mini-retreat with a pad of paper and some art supplies. I felt that I needed to get lost in order to find myself again.

As I walked through the woods that day, I opened up to hearing what I wasn't able to in town, surrounded by people. I uncovered resentment I'd been holding onto and through my art I was able to see myself letting go of some things I didn't realize I had been carrying. I was also able to reclaim lost aspects of myself I had pushed aside in favor of powering through difficult points in life. It was like dismantling a structure that had been erected in a haphazard way and reclaiming vital pillars I could use to reconstruct a more stable and authentic worldview for myself and those I cared about.

You can see examples of my personal creative expression that were the results of this exercise on the following pages.

Bones that I chose to surrender and release included...

- All of the expectations people outside of me had planted inside of me.

- All of the judgments that I allowed to influence my self view.

- All of the chatter that gnaws away on the inside of me and makes me feel less than whole.

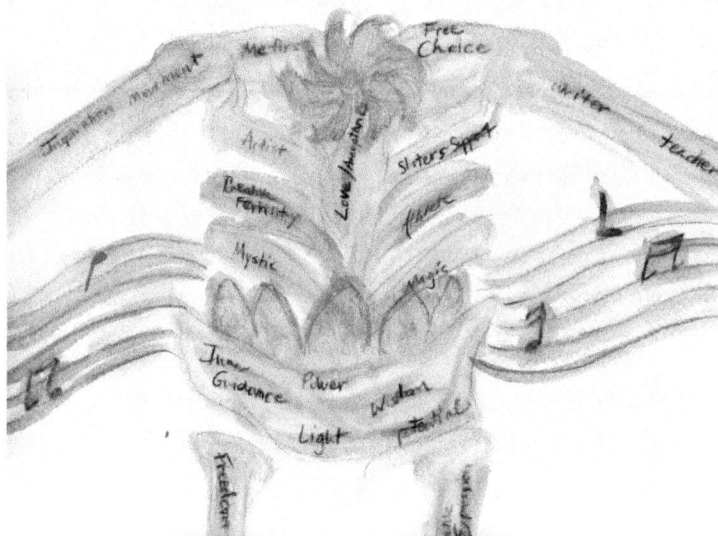

The bones I found buried deep inside of me and then reclaimed that day were my...

- light

- spirit

- true self

- potential

- sense of possibility and freedom

- authenticity

- inner guidance and self-direction

It's not necessary to take yourself out in nature to do this exercise, but it can be helpful to reconnect there if possible. A simple change of scenery can make room for new possibilities. Feel free to do what works best for you so that you can get back in touch with your own answers, but do treat yourself with tenderness and respect.

Let's move into the exercise now by reflecting on what this has brought up for you.

PREPARATION STEP 3:
Gathering the Bones

🔊))

Sit still in a quiet place. Put your hands over your heart and breath several deep breaths.

Recall a time of love or gratitude and feel what it was like to be there. Feel it as if it were happening in this very moment. Let that feeling flow over your entire body and as you breathe, let it expand until it surrounds the room, this space, this area, this region, this country, and this planet.

Then ask your heart to show you your own cemetery. In response, you might receive images, words, sounds, feelings or something else. Just notice what is happening and tune into what it feels like to be walking in this cemetery of yours. Stay connected here and open your eyes to answer the following questions with your NON-Dominant hand:

1. What symbolic "bones" will you be surrendering and releasing on the funeral pyre today? These are the things that no longer serve you that you choose to surrender and leave behind.

2. What symbolic "bones" are you willing to reclaim today? These would be the symbolic aspects of you or things that you will reclaim and use to rebuild yourself.

3. Create a symbolic representation of what you're leaving behind. Be creative. Let your inner heartist out to draw, paint, sing, dance. Create some type of expression of the "bones" you are leaving behind and those you are gathering. What's important here is the experience of creating and expressing rather than what the end product looks like.

These simple exercises have the power to get to the heart of the matter and you've moved through a lot of internal work by doing them. You've taken a look at the broad cultural implications of self sacrifice, moved on to see these through the lens of your own experience, and made decisions about what inner dialogues you need to release and what inner resources you need to claim. This inner work is every bit as valuable and takes as much if not more courage than the external work you can see with your own eyes. While some of what you've discovered you probably knew on some level, seeing it on paper can be a moving experience. Acknowledge yourself for moving through this, for having the courage to step into the unfamiliar and for trusting what came out. Even though these are intensely personal experiences, sharing how this was for you inside the community can assist you even more in claiming what you discovered. No pressure to do this, no right or wrong, simply an option available to you. Listen to what your heart says, and follow the guidance it gives you.

Next we'll use this deep internal work you've done to
gain a new perspective, seeing your commitments with fresh eyes.

CHAPTER 5
Exploration

---

*"When you know what drains you
and fuels you, THAT's self-care."*

HILLARY RUBIN

At this point, you're probably eager to see how this is going to play out in your life and I am too! This is an exciting time filled with hope, curiosity and a sense of possibility for what lies before you. Getting a chance to clear the slate can be invigorating on its own and doing so with both your mindset and your commitments can amplify the enthusiasm. Yet before we get going we need to take a moment and address the inevitable: before things get better, they might get worse. Your life will likely feel more intense as you recognize the need for change and take steps outside of what's been familiar. You'll encounter resistance from yourself as you move through these next steps that prepare you and you'll likely also encounter it from those around you who will be impacted by the changes you choose to make. The important thing here is that you approach this as an experiment and with a sense of curiosity. You're giving yourself a brief time, 30 days, to commit to experiencing life differently. When you feel reluctant, ask yourself: *How will I know what is possible in my life if I don't try something different?*

Many women hesitate and think, "I can't let go of this for 30 days! If I'm not there to do it, who will?" Well I'm here to promise you that the world will not fall apart just because it is deprived of your constant attention for 30 days. And honestly, if we were to know the true balance of your contributions, I'm certain that you've paid this forward over the course of your life. If I could give every woman a complete month off from all responsibilities, I would love to make that happen, but the *Sabbatical from "Yes"* isn't calling for that. It's a gentle way to give yourself a rest, to give you more of your time and attention so that you can top up your energy reserves. You won't be letting go of everything in your life, but rather just making some adjustments, which can still feel tricky. Even so, they are absolutely possible.

When you're setting up your Sabbatical from "Yes," having conversations with key people in your life to ask for their assistance and support can increase your confidence and commitment to seeing it through, which in turn will assist in making the experience smoother for you and everyone else involved. This could be new and uncomfortable at first, but a necessary step, especially if the plan you create requires assistance from these people. That's where the power of brainstorming comes into play. Either grab a friend to brainstorm options with or put your situation out to the online community and ask for suggestions. Together, we can think of creative solutions to any situation.

I've seen it work over and over in the lives of women and men. There have been people who have decided through their Energy Matrix to let go of certain responsibilities as part of their sabbatical. They have made arrangements for other people in their lives to handle things such as house cleaning and laundry by trading time with a housemate for something they enjoy doing more. They felt relief as they delegated aspects of their professional life that were draining their energy to their colleagues whom embraced stepping up to the challenge. They have let go of volunteer positions that required much of their time and energy, and stopped saying 'yes' to feeling obligated to schedule meetings at inconvenient times. What you will let go of and what your sabbatical will look like depends entirely on what you're going to discover as you complete these next preparation steps, so let's channel that eager anticipation or transmute any apprehension or fear coming up by taking a couple of deep breaths.

The next step is to complete the Energy Matrix.

PREPARATION STEP FOUR:
Energy Matrix

🔊))

The Energy Matrix is your tool for logging all of the commitments and tense situations that you currently have and running them through a thorough evaluation to determine how much energy each of them returns to you. You'll check in with your heart to see what it has to say about them and begin generating options for making decisions about how you will modify or release those that are not serving you.

In case you just started sweating, shaking or panicking, let me stop for a moment to assure you that even though you might think the world will stop if you adjust all of your patterns of doing, I stand here (sit here, really) typing this for you and I'm living proof that the world will not end. I've been through this process myself as have all of the *Self-Full Living* participants and mentor clients before you. YOU will change, but the world will not end. In fact, it will be a better place because of it — trust me!

I think a virtual hug might be in order right now, so wrap your arms around yourself for a second, take a deep breath and...

<<<< s q u e e z e >>>>>

There now, let's get back to it, because I think you'll like this next part.

What you'll get out of this sabbatical can be compared to magical powers. Here are just a few reasons why you'll LOVE taking this sabbatical and might even consider making it permanent:

- You'll be giving yourself a break (chances are you need one). The time that you gain from letting go of things that weren't an authentic 'yes' can now be directed toward self-full activities that actually energize you.

- You'll take an opportunity to re-align your commitments with your authentic 'yes,' or at least take a break from them while you confirm that they are an authentic 'yes.'

- When you say "no" to others you'll be able to do that because of the bigger "yes" that is building inside of you. Turns out, when we pause our impulsive "yes" to others, we actually give ourselves the space and permission to express a more authentic "yes" to ourselves, to our own desires and preferences.

- You'll follow a new protocol for all requests that is super easy:

  ◊ When a request is made of you and an instant response is required, you say something like this: **"No."**

  ◊ If you aren't comfortable with that response, you can say **"Thanks for thinking of me, but no thanks."**

  ◊ If it's something you would normally agree to and you still feel compelled to provide an explanation, you can say, **"I'd love to, but I'm taking a sabbatical from (insert appropriate phrase: volunteering, helping, taking on more responsibility, etc) and focusing on self care right now. Maybe next time."**

  ◊ If it's something that you think you'd really like doing, ask for time to consider it, preferably 30 days until you complete the sabbatical. At that point, you'll be able see with more clarity what you're wanting in your life.

Let's move on to complete the Energy Matrix.

Energy Matrix Sheet 🔊

Commitments or Responsibilities	Body	Ease	Enthusiasm	Thinking	Total	Direction

STEP 1: Document the Commitments

Create a list of your current commitments and responsibilities and put them on each line. Remember to include the situations that you called out in earlier exercises or any situations that are both a source of tension and/or joy for you. You'll want to hone in on situations in which you habitually say 'yes,' but wish you had said 'no,' or where you silently comply with something you don't want.

Be aware that even when filling your schedule with things that you love and projects that excite you, it's possible to over-commit and slip into overwhelm. Once you've completed the Energy Matrix, you'll have more clarity about what is giving you energy and what is not. Once you've experienced your *Sabbatical from "Yes,"* then I suspect you'll crave that spaciousness and have a different perspective when making future commitments. From there, you can make decisions that are energizing and include more space and time for you to continually recharge.

STOP HERE and complete your list.

STEP 2: Rate the Commitments

Take a moment. Put your hands over your heart and breathe several deep breaths.

Recall a time of love or gratitude and feel what it was like to be there. Feel it in this moment. Let that feeling flow over your entire body and as you breathe, let it expand until it surrounds the room, this space, this area, this region, this country, this planet. Then open your eyes and continue through the next steps.

4.   Take the first item on your list. Get into the feeling state of actually meeting the commitment in this moment.

5.   Rate your item in the matrix based on the scales on the following page.

6.   Repeat the above 2 steps for each item on your list until you have completed the above process for all of them.

7.   Add up your answers for each commitment and record in the total column.

BODY

Tense	Somewhat	Neutral	Somewhat	Relaxed
1	2	3	4	5

EASE

Frustration	Somewhat	Neutral	Somewhat	Ease
1	2	3	4	5

ENTHUSIASM

Boredom	Somewhat	Neutral	Somewhat	Excitement
1	2	3	4	5

THOUGHTS

Negative	Somewhat	Neutral	Somewhat	Positive
1	2	3	4	5

NOTE: *If you're struggling with the Energy Matrix or something doesn't feel quite "on" here for you, then you might be at a point in life where you don't have a lot of external responsibilities and don't feel overcommitted, or you interpret your situation differently. For example, you might realize that instead of seeing it as taking a sabbatical from saying "yes" to others, it might be more productive for you to take a sabbatical from saying "no" to yourself. If this is so, take a slightly different approach to the Energy Matrix and the sabbatical. Rather than filling it with external commitments and responsibilities, you'll be listing the things you are desiring in your life, but that you're saying "no" to. Think of it as your heart of heart's wish list. In your case, you'll modify your Sabbatical from "Yes" to focus on a Sabbatical from "No." It's an opportunity to practice for 30 days saying "Yes" to yourself. It will have the same result, only your entry point for getting there is different. Your list would include things, situations, desires, etc. in which you are constantly saying 'no' to but deeply desire in your life. For example, you might have a deep desire to take an art class, but keep putting it off for a myriad of reasons, or it might be a different career path you want to explore, or a travel experience, etc. If you've flipped the sabbatical, begin thinking about how you can practice saying 'yes' to yourself more and use this as your guide to complete the following sections.*

STEP 3: Determine the Direction

After completing the matrix, you'll fill out the "Direction" column. Take the results of what you entered for each situation into meditation for guidance. Ask your heart to show you which commitments you will keep and which commitments you will release (even temporarily). Get into the feeling state of each commitment.

1. First imagine keeping it and what that feels like. "K"

2. Next imagine releasing it and what that feels like. "R"

3. Choose the one that feels most expansive

4. Sometimes neither "K" nor "R" feel right and in those cases, enter "M" for modify and we'll review that during the next section.

5. Enter "K" for keep, "R" for release, or "M" for modify in the last column "Direction."

Congratulations! You've completed the basics for the sabbatical and are ready to brainstorm options for the rows where you entered "R" or "M." These items form the core of what you'll be taking a rest from during your own version of the *Sabbatical from "Yes."*

If you're tempted to power through and continue to the next section, I'd encourage you to take at least a small break to stretch and get some fresh air. You've just completed a major chunk of work here and the next part will require a fresh perspective.

STEP 4: Brainstorming Options

Review each "M" and "R" item on your list. Some will require a little brainstorming for creative options of how to best handle the situation. It might take time to gain clarity, but can be easier by recruiting the help of creative friends or members of our online community.

It's worth noting that if you go into this with an open mind, being open to new possibilities of how you can get your needs met as well as the other person or organization, then you will be primed to see options that you haven't considered before or even thought existed.

Follow these brainstorming guidelines:

1. Gather at least 25 ideas of how you can adjust these commitments or situations so that they will be more enjoyable for you and give you more energy. Some will only require you to make a choice. Others might include additional support from another person or people.

2. Accept all options and suggestions. Collect all of the ideas that are presented to you without judging or evaluating, regardless of how odd or other worldly they might seem.

3. Review all of the suggestions and identify the one that resonates most with you and seems to best fit the situation.

The grid on the following page will give you
a place to start as you brainstorm.

Commitments	Ideas

As you continue to make decisions that are in tune with your inner wisdom and nourish you, you're going to build up a balance of choices that return energy to you, rather than drain you. That soulful, tuned in experience of honoring your inner wisdom, and making wise and compassionate choices that nourish you is what I call exquisite self-care. Let's dig into that a bit so we can discover what it looks like for you.

Each time we say 'yes' when we really mean 'no,' we violate our truth and create discord in ourselves with others. It's a form of self-betrayal and despite the likely intent to benefit someone, sadly nobody benefits from it. When we take two of the most precious resources we have, our time and our integrity, and insert someone else's priority above our own, we end up lower on the priority list and feel the weight of obligation that breeds resentment. When we are living this way the people around us, including the children we care about, live life without the most important gift that we can give, the gift of our full presence and the best example that we can model for their future.

We might be able to justify that we're doing something for the good of our family, for the good of our organization or community, because we want to be nice, we want to avoid conflict, be liked, or (insert your favorite excuse here). But, what we are really doing is modeling a lie. We are modeling that:

- It's okay to be out of alignment with who we really are.

- We are not worthy of what we want.

- We must twist and contort ourselves to meet another's expectations, putting aside our own truth.

- This is what adults do.

- This is what we wish for the future.

This is important work you're doing and when you do this, EVERYONE around you benefits by your example.

Now, a bit more about what to expect before we move forward...

Expect to use the word "no" much more often during this period than you might have in the past. You're giving yourself a rest from saying "yes" to others, so during this sabbatical you'll be declining offers to take on new responsibilities and new commitments, even if the thought of this makes you cringe. The fact is, you already have enough on your plate and in our modern world, it's up to each one of us to create our own boundaries. Regardless of whether or not you're feeling guilty or proud about how you've handled your existing commitments up to this point, you'd probably agree with me that it's time for a break (or you wouldn't have gotten this far in the book). **Nobody is going to tap you on the shoulder and offer this up to you. If it's ever going to happen, it's something you've got to give to rise up and claim, something only you can give to yourself.** Trust me, it's much more fun to do this proactively than relying on a relationship, health or financial crisis to force you to step back and reevaluate. As you create a bit of elbow room in your life and sense the spaciousness, your discomfort will subside and you'll be able to relax a bit, breathe easier, and get back in touch with your inner wisdom.

While this is a sabbatical from saying "yes" to others, it's also a sabbatical from saying "no" to yourself. You'll find that through this process you'll learn how to shift your "yes" from the external environment, back toward yourself. You'll feel more in tune with your inner drive and you'll be using your authentic "yes" to meet your own needs, rather than the needs of others.

As you launch your sabbatical and start implementing the Weekly Action Guide, you can expect more ease and congruence in your life, and to feel greater clarity and higher levels of energy. As you move through the actions and reflections, you'll reconnect with your inner wisdom. Many women report feeling more confident, connected and relaxed. In fact, you might decide you like living this way and choose to make this new normal a part of your life. If that's the case, you'll want to brainstorm more permanent options for keeping those aspects in place long term.

CHAPTER 6
Launching Your Sabbatical

"What we manifest in our lives is a reflection of what is deep inside us: our beliefs about our own worth, our right to happiness, what we deserve in life. When those beliefs change, so does our life."

ROBIN NORWOOD

---

ere we are, you've done the reflection, the examination and the brainstorming. You have set yourself up for your Sabbatical and are ready to start. This is the part that takes the most courage. So just before we take that step to launch your sabbatical, I'd like to share a story to illustrate what this experience looked like through the eyes of my first client.

By the Fall of 2012 I had been collecting resources and tools, and doing research on how I could create a course that would simulate this process for women, but I was scared shitless to actually pull it together and offer it to the world. As an introvert with a rich inner life, it almost didn't seem necessary to share it with others, but for my work to make a difference in the world, sharing was a requirement.

Then one day, I told a friend about what I had been working on and just saying it out loud to someone besides my coach or my mastermind group felt fantastic. A few months later, that same friend experienced a breakup and realized that she had invested most of her energy in her ex, leaving little for herself. When she asked me to assist her in getting her life back, I attempted to send her links for the resources I was gathering. But she told me this wasn't going to work for her; she wanted my active assistance to find her way through the emptiness in her life, and to recover her sense of self and inner guidance.

Can a person feel reluctantly excited? If so, I was as close to that as possible. It felt divinely inspired, so I pushed my doubts aside and stretched outside of my comfort zone in agreement. We decided to meet weekly for eight weeks. She became my muse and week by week, I would tune into divine guidance to craft the next week's focus, using the exercises, articles, experiences, tools, etc. that I had been gathering. During the second week, the step was the *Sabbatical from*

"*Yes,*" and the bulk of the process you'll be going through was written. Week by week, the *Self-Full Living Framework* was constructed and I saw her life change before my eyes. She regained her spark, she let go of things that were draining her and reconnected with who she was, reigniting her inner worth and her inner light. What has resulted, in the years since, has been astounding. She's in a creative flow and has written two books, and lyrics to songs flow through her like a fountain. She has stepped out of her comfort zone to offer workshops of her own, do public speaking and share who she is with the world. She's even sharing the stage at an event this year with someone she's admired from a distance for years. She's a constant inspiration to me and those around her and she traces this renaissance period back to her experience with her own *Sabbatical from "Yes."*

"Self-Full Living *was a BIG part of who I am today.
I'm so in touch with my intrinsic worth, it's crazy!
I'm authentic and set better boundaries, limiting
my commitments and doing only things that give me
energy. I worry less and have made space for more
nurturing friends. I'm infinitely grateful.*"

BONNIE O'BOYLE

Since then I've had women in their twenties all the way to their sixties take the *Self-Full Living* course and get profound results. I'm moved by the changes that I see and the moments when they realize that they don't have to live life the way they had assumed, they have more options and more space to be who they are and to live their lives congruently.

"I have come to understand more fully my body's healthiest desires, needs and messages...(and) tune into those messages I did not even know how to hear in the past. This listening is helping me change or redirect my decisions so that I am experiencing more and more of my health and Wholeness. (I've) become more aware of priorities in my day to day life that strengthen my whole self, so that I am becoming a stronger and more capable person in my job, relationships and even fun stuff."

ANNETTE OLSEN

Each woman who embarks on this journey has the same resistance as you, and her courage is what gets her through. You may find it easier to muster up courage to defend someone you love or to do what needs to be done to assist in a life threatening situation but that same courage can also be called upon as you step out of your comfort zone, risk getting messy and not doing things perfectly. There's a courageous, adventurous part of you and that's the part to call on now as we move forward.

So now it's time to launch your sabbatical!

There are three parts to launching:

1. Take action

2. Declare your worth

3. Celebrate

STEP 1: Take Action

Take action within 24 hours on the commitments you've made to release the hold that the expectations of others have on you. Even if it can only be a micro action in the direction you have chosen, take the step forward: Draft your resignation letters and sabbatical notifications, have those conversations, write a letter or email. Do what needs to be done.

It's always helpful to approach this from a place of gratitude for what the experience brought into your life and with compassion for the person, organization, etc. receiving the notification of what you're releasing. Take one step toward releasing each item on your list by letting **someone else know** about your decision. Give those involved the next week or two to ask questions, get turnover information from you, and plan for your absence. In some cases that absence might require extensive planning. Handle these on a case-by-case basis.

Once you have your plans in place and have solidified options and recruited the support you need for the modifications, then you are ready to review the *Declaration of Worth*.

Step 2: Declare Your Worth

The *Declaration of Worth* gives voice to what you are reclaiming and it's imperative that it's in alignment with your highest vision for yourself. I encourage you to stretch, but also honor what's going on inside of you. Your "yes" has immense value and from this day forward through the next 30 days you'll be carefully considering what receives the honor of your "yes." Your *Declaration of Worth* in integral to the foundation of your sabbatical, and is deserving of your consideration and consciousness before you go ahead and sign it or create your own version.

1.   Locate your *Wanted Poster* on page 60 and review your new mantra at the bottom

2.   Locate the *Declaration of Worth* on page 95 and read it through.

3.   What questions do you have about it?

4.   What was your body's response to it?

     ◊   Tightness?

     ◊   Relaxation?

     ◊   Notice something else?

5.   Take 24 hours to let the Declaration of Worth soak in and ponder making this commitment. Take it into meditation; ask for guidance, make sure this is something that you are 100% behind before you say 'yes' to it.

If, after reading it and after taking it into meditation, you have a 'no,' that's also great! We are looking for alignment and we will allow your 'no' to direct us. You have the opportunity to create your own version of the Declaration to which you can say a wholehearted "yes." Remember to stretch. You want to be on the **outer edge of your "yes."** To create your own version, reflect back on the exercises you have already completed to look for words and phrases that you can include. Reconnect with your new mantra from the Wanted Poster exercise. Once you're at a place where you think you've got it down, go back to step #4 and sit with it overnight. Once you've got a confirmation that this is complete, then proceed to the next step.

A word about finding your authentic "yes." Some would say that in order to have a "yes" it needs to feel good in your body, but that's not always the case. Sometimes our body signals fear of the unknown, while still being an authentic "yes." If you're struggling to recognize your authentic "yes," you can return to a time in your life when you felt deep resonance with someone or something that you know without a doubt was an authentic "yes" for you. Get into the feeling state of that person or experience. Notice what you feel in your body. Most likely there will be a sense of expansion or opening with an authentic "yes." Even if your body is signaling fear of the unknown, it can still be an authentic "yes" if the fear associated is the type of fear that has an expansive quality to it, such as stepping into a larger version of yourself or inhabiting more space. When comparing this to a sacred 'no', your body for a 'no' is typically compressed and constricted, it has a shrinking quality to it. If all of this sounds like greek to you, you are not alone. In the 30 day guide, you'll be practicing daily to hone in on your own body's 'yes' and 'no' signals. If you're stumped here, go with your best guess for now. Remember, we are experimenting and you will discover more clarity as we move forward.

Now that you have a *Declaration of Worth* to which you can authentically say 'yes,' you are ready to take your sabbatical!

This is it, the moment all of this initial effort has been leading up to, and it's time to commit your signature, to take your stand for yourself and by extension, humanity. If you're using the version of Declaration of Worth in this book, you can download and print a version at **www.christidaniels.com/goodies.** If you created your own version, print that out now.

Declaration of Worth

From this day forward, I claim my worth.
I claim my full self, my beauty, my shadow,
my love, my anger and everything in between.
From this day forward, I cease agreement with
saying 'yes' to anything that I do not want.

I reject the notion that...

...my worth exists only when I do something for someone else.

...it is my job to be responsible for anyone else's happiness.

...I must agree with someone's opinion to keep the peace.

...I must cooperate or collaborate against my inner will.

...I must give up anything for another person
to have what they want.

...I must scrape bare the walls of my soul
for any reason, whatsoever.

...I am here to advance anyone else's agenda
at the expense of my own light.

Rather, I embrace the truth that I have a special gift to share in this world.

I might not be fully aware of what that is in this moment, but I know it resides inside of me.

It resides inside EACH of us.

It is my mission to BE my most authentic, unique BEing.

If I neglect myself, this will not be possible.

If I say 'yes' when I mean 'no,' I am not authentic.

I embrace the truth that what is best for my highest self is best for everyone, that truly helping myself helps everyone

Therefore, I only say 'yes' and choose things that nurture me and stoke my internal flame.

I am the only one who can make that choice.

I understand that the divine speaks through my curiosity, my yearnings and my excitement.

I embrace situations where I feel the energy of satisfaction, fulfillment and pleasure.

I embrace silence and nurturing time for myself.

I trust my inner guidance to show me the way.

I am worthy in each moment, simply because I exist.

I am valuable, simply because I exist.
I embrace and hold sacred my gift of life.

I embrace me FULLY.

I am enough and perfect, just as

I AM.

_____

Signed

_____

Date

My *Sabbatical from "Yes"* starts on: ____/____/____
and ends on ____/____/____ (30-Days later)

This declaration comes with an auto-renewal at expiration, until
such time as you should choose to say yes to something different.

The initial term for your sabbatical will be 30 days, however, it might make more sense for you to take a longer break. Trust your inner wisdom and make the choice that is right for you.

Sign your Declaration of Worth and insert today's date
and the date for the end of your sabbatical.

As you embark on this journey, I'll share with you the most valuable lesson I learned in my sixteen years of corporate experience, in the hope that it might serve you in the next 30 days and beyond. It's based on a famous saying, "*It's better to beg for forgiveness, than to ask for permission,*" attributed to Grace Murray Hopper. She was an American computer scientist and U.S. Navy Rear Admiral. Hearing this mantra over and over again, I understood it to mean that I had implicit permission to do as I thought best and that I should proceed to follow my conscience, that stopping to ask for permission implied that I did not have the authority to make the decision and was bound to someone else for direction. Further, if I encountered resistance from others for my actions, I could always apologize but my initial belief in my decision would not be sacrificed. I applied this principle so many times during my career and even when moving into the tent. I didn't ask permission from the company I worked with to telecommute from a random field that summer. To this day there are only two people in that company who know about it (well, maybe more if they read this book.) It was the right thing to do for me and since it didn't impact them at all, I heeded Grace Murray Hopper's call and let my knowing of what was right lead the way.

The fact that YOU are the one living your life implies that you have sovereignty over it. **You need never ask for permission from someone else to do what's right for you.** You do not need their blessing, you do not require their agreement. (Pausing for a moment, let me say here that I'm referring to choices that do not involve harming another person. I wouldn't condone that and you wouldn't use this in that way, but it needed to be said.) When you live your life as the CEO of it, you'll be responsible for each and every decision, each and every outcome, good and bad, but there's power in taking responsibility for your life. There's power in assuming you have your own permission to do so, to make the choices that are right for you in any given moment. There's power in declaring your worth, in giving time to yourself to enjoy life, to get clear on what's important to you, to reconnect with your inner wisdom.

Now as you step forward into that power, it's time to ...

Celebrate!

A glass of sparkling cider, water or champagne
might be in order right now!

Here's to YOU!

You have joined the ranks of women all over the world waking up to their own power to influence the course of their life and to make their highest contribution to the world. By treating your time and energy with the utmost respect, and letting your inner authority be your guide, you're on your way to being a ruthless, big-hearted, badass lover of yourself and those entrusted in your care. Our world will be a better place because of what you're choosing to give to yourself. I'm honored and humbled by your commitment and courage, and I'm eager to hear about your experiments.

Celebrate by sharing your start and stop dates in the online community, with your local group or close friends. Remember that you'll want support and accountability; it makes the experience much easier and more fun!

Now, time to check out the 30-Day Action Guide
for your weekly actions and reflections.

CHAPTER 7
30-Day Action Guide

"One of the reasons I live such a fantastic life is because I pay attention…. Everything is trying to take you home to yourself and when you're home with yourself, when you're solidly there connected to whatever you call creation, even if you don't call it anything, connected to an energy source that has unlimited power for you, you are your best."

OPRAH WINFREY

Excited... curious... anxious... hopeful... The feelings likely coursing through you right now are complex and normal. When we choose to take on something new, to try a different way, the "unknown" can feel uncomfortable. Rather than relying on how you've approached things in the past, your next 30 Days will be ones of discovery, of embracing the unknown and becoming more willing to move through discomfort as it shows up. Having completed all of the inner and outer work to give yourself this sabbatical, your choice to do this work is firmly rooted in self-awareness and compassion. You've tapped into alignment and what's true for you and thus, into a power that can see you through anything you might encounter here. As you move forward with these next few weeks, see this as your opportunity to claim a new way of operating in the world for yourself. It's carving out a new path and a new way of being that will be specifically designed to honor who you are, and residing inside of that is immeasurable power and potential for goodness. Your coming days will be both sacred and irreverent, so know that whatever is showing up, regardless of how you perceive it, it contains beautiful golden nuggets of wisdom for you.

SCHEDULE

This guide contains actions and reflections for each day of your sabbatical. Remember, you can download a PDF copy of the guide at www.christidaniels.com/goodies if you would like more room for notes or simply wish to not make notes in your book. Each day will take you 30 minutes or less to complete. Completing these questions every day will give you the greatest experience and thus the greatest benefits from your sabbatical. Don't overlook them. Commit to them. Set a recurring appointment time on your calendar for a daily "date" with yourself to complete the questions. The simplicity and engagement with them are where the real shifts occur and I know you want the results. You'll deepen your connection and awareness of your personal power, your inner wisdom, self-worth, and preferences that return energy to you and nourish you at higher levels.

Let's jump in!

WEEK ONE
Embody Power

"Clarity comes from engagement, not thought."

MARIE FORLEO

This week we will be combining the power of our biochemistry with gratitude. You'll start each day energized and end each day with a grateful heart. These are two activities that will serve as bookends or anchors to your day for the duration of your sabbatical. Set your alarm to wake up twenty minutes earlier than normal. As soon as you get up, strike a power pose for two minutes, then follow it with a brisk 15 minute walk, preferably outside. If walking outside isn't an option, you could jump on the rebounder, jump rope, climb up and down stairs or put on some music and dance like nobody's watching. The point here is to get your body moving for at least 15 minutes immediately following your power pose.

What's a power pose? It's any stance that you take that is placing your body in an open position, such as:

- Your arms on your hips, legs hip width apart, shoulders back, head high. If you can imagine the pose of the Jolly Green Giant or Wonder Woman, you've got it.

- Leaning back in your chair with your hands behind your head and your feet propped up on your desk.

Amy Cuddy, a Social Psychologist and Professor at Harvard Business School, says that certain "power poses" change how people perceive you as well as actually changing your body chemistry. Just two minutes in a power pose can increase your testosterone level, positioning you for taking risks. It also decreases levels of cortisol, the "stress hormone," setting you up for more calm and powerful interactions with others, without the need for sacrificing who you are.

The opposite was also found to be true. Assuming "low power" positions by closing or compressing the body, in effect shrinking, created the reverse effect in body chemistry.

Cuddy and her research partner proved that our bodies can change our minds, our minds can change our behavior and our behavior can change our outcomes.

Why walk or move for 15 minutes?

Walking is a gentle way to move your body so it can tap into it's ability to produce feel-good neurochemicals such as serotonin and dopamine, as well as create an endorphin rush. It's a great way to start your day feeling energized, so that you can enjoy whatever you choose to do and have access to higher levels of thinking, creativity and focus.

Don't stop at day 7, make this a daily habit for the next 30 days.

With this simple start to your day you will be building up an empowered and more energized state of being as you move through the world. It might seem strange to think of doing a power pose, walking and moving as empowering and energizing you, but that's exactly what happens. Your body is your vehicle for getting around on the planet and when you inhabit a larger space with power poses and when you choose to move it around and tap into your inner wealth of beneficial hormones, you are taking up more space in the world. You are sending the message to yourself and others that you are comfortable being in your own skin. You're training yourself to take actions that benefit you in positive ways. Doing this step alone can help boost your mood, energy and improve your outlook, but we aren't going to stop there. We're going to link this with the steps you'll encounter over the next few weeks to create a synergistic effect, a mind-body-spirit cocktail of empowering goodness.

Beyond these next 30 mornings, you might also choose to do a power pose in a discrete location before a negotiation, speaking in public, going to a networking meeting or an interview. This ensures that the most powerful and confident aspects of you show through when you need them.

I also highly recommend watching Amy Cuddy's TED Talk, Your Body Language Shapes Who You Are. You can find the link on the resource page at **www.christidaniels.com/goodies.**

Track your progress with Daily Check-ins

Week One	1	2	3	4	5	6	7
Power Pose & Walk							
Gratitude							

1. What are you grateful for today?

2. What has been happening in your life that went well today?

3. Where did friction show up today?

4. What was the most powerful part of your day?

5. (At the end of the week) What is different about your life this week compared to last week?

WEEK TWO
Reconnect with Your Inner Wisdom

"Your body is a wonderful, wonderful source of information – information that no one else in the world can give you. Your therapist can't do it, your body worker can't do it. Your body is an expert on you. She or he has more information to give you about yourself than anyone or anything else in the world."

KATHLEEN DESMAISONS, PH.D.
AND AUTHOR OF POTATOES NOT PROZAC

This week your daily action will be to reconnect with your inner knowing by getting in touch with your body. Sometimes we become so unaware of what is going on within our bodies that we ignore the signals they're trying to send. These signals contain valuable information to assist us in understanding if something is adding to our energy or depleting it.

I'm reminded of a short promotional video from the organization **Go Red for Women** called *Just a Little Heart Attack*. It stars and was directed by Emmy-nominated Elizabeth Banks and it's a smart, if somewhat uncomfortable, clip of a morning in one busy woman's life. In it she continues to ignore all of the signals that her body is sending her that she needs to slow down until she finds herself on the floor, calling 9-1-1 to say she thinks she had "just a little heart attack."

There are a variety of reasons why we disconnect from our bodies, perhaps as many as there are women. Our mission this week is to reconnect with this most glorious vehicle that gets us around on planet earth. At bedtime, right before you end your day, tune into your body. See if there is a situation that applies to the scenarios below. If so, bring that situation back into your mind and put yourself into the feeling place of it, as if you're reliving the experience.

Then, answer the questions on the following pages. Remember to be specific. This will become a daily habit as well for the remaining portion of your **30 days.**

Before you start your week, I highly recommend watching the video yourself. It will deepen your understanding of what ignoring your body signals can look like in daily life and you'll find the link at **www.christidaniels.com/goodies.**

Track your progress with Daily Check-ins

Week Two	8	9	10	11	12	13	14
Power Pose & Walk							
Gratitude							
Body Check-in							

Answer these questions for your Daily Body Check-ins

When did you say, think, agree or do something even though you felt inside that you wanted something else for yourself?	What sensations did you notice in your body when this happened?
When did you say, think, agree or do something that was good for you, but disappointed someone else?	What sensations did you notice in your body when this happened?
When did you stay in integrity on the outside and the inside, and it felt good?	What sensations did you notice in your body when this happened?
What are you noticing overall about your body's 'no' sensations?	What are you noticing overall about your body's 'yes' sensations?

WEEK THREE
Reconnect with Your Intrinsic Worth

"The most meaningful lesson I learned from being at death's door is that unless I love myself, nothing else in my life can function at its best. The amount of depth, meaning, and joy I experience in my life is in direct proportion to how much love I have for myself. And, unsurprisingly, the amount of love, respect, support, and compassion I receive from others is also in direct proportion to how much of the same I have for myself."

ANITA MOORJANI

This week you will read the *Declaration of Worth* on page 95 or your own custom version out loud each morning. As you're doing this, move beyond the fact that you're reading the words and connect with the feeling of your words. As you say them, imagine every cell of your body is saying them and feel what that's like. Truly embody your reading, have your full body say the words with you. Then make note of your answers to the questions below.

Make a note below of the sensations you noticed in your body while you were saying the *Declaration of Worth*.

1.   What are you noticing about your body's 'yes' sensations? (Describe the sensation and the location.)

2.   What are you noticing about your body's 'no' sensations? (Describe the sensation and the location.)

Track your progress with Daily Check-ins

Week Three	15	16	17	18	19	20	21
Power Pose & Walk							
Gratitude							
Body Check-in							
Declaration of Worth							

Answer these questions for your Daily Body Check-ins

When did you say, think, agree or do something even though you felt inside that you wanted something else for yourself?	What sensations did you notice in your body when this happened?
When did you say, think, agree or do something that was good for you, but disappointed someone else?	What sensations did you notice in your body when this happened?
When did you stay in integrity on the outside and the inside and it felt good?	What sensations did you notice in your body when this happened?
What are you noticing overall about your body's 'no' sensations?	What are you noticing overall about your body's 'yes' sensations?

At the end of your week, answer these questions:

1. What are you grateful for this week?

2. What do you notice about your days this week compared to last?

WEEK FOUR
Stabilize Your Rhythm

---

*"My morning workout ritual is the most basic form
of self-reliance; it reminds me that, when all else fails,
I can at least depend on myself."*

TWYLA THARP

Time to focus on stability and rhythms that support you living your life with your energy tank on full. It's the foundation for your inner and outer strength. A daily routine of grounding and energizing activities contributes to an optimum state for your body-mind-soul system. If you compared waking up and starting off your day to a morning commute by car, a typical day might include hopping into your car, pointing it in the direction you want to go and driving it there. Now, imagine what would happen if you never stopped to check to see if you had enough gas, oil, or if your tires were inflated. At some point, your car would stop going... until you took the time to fill it back up again.

When it comes to our bodies, we are often capable of keeping ourselves going and ignoring very important signals that tell us our energy level is on low, or that something is wrong that needs to be addressed (like in the *Just a Little Heart Attack* video.) Pushing ourselves while we are on empty is like pushing our car down the street when it's out of gas. It requires an incredible amount of energy. Even when armed with

---

a case of energy drinks or coffee at our side, we're likely to end up with an injury, accident, illness or whatever it takes so that our bodies eventually get the rest we need. For some of us, this is a cycle that repeats and ends up being a rhythm that deconstructs us over time, rather than one that nourishes us and builds us up. Our goal here is to be living with a full tank, so that you're confident, feeling great, and have extra energy overflowing to those you love and the projects you're passionate about.

Reflecting back on your life, what things have you noticed that set you up for a fabulous day? They might be things you enjoy, that make you laugh or that just make your day extra special when they happen.

List at least seven of them below.

1. _____

2. _____

3. _____

4. _____

5. _____

6. _____

7. _____

View this list as your custom menu and return here daily to choose at least one thing to do each day. We're both raising the bar here on your energy reserves and we're taking tiny steps toward nurturing. Getting accustomed to having a higher level of energy and a sense of normalcy when it comes to having fun and receiving nurturing will all assist you in stabilizing at a new, higher level of operating. You've got dreams and desires stirring in your soul and this higher energy level will be incredibly beneficial as you start exploring them.

(Make this FUN, it's like getting an assignment to do something that you really REALLY enjoy)!

Track your progress with Daily Check-ins

Week Four	22	23	24	25	26	27	28
Power Pose & Walk							
Gratitude							
Body Check-in							
Energy Boost from Your Custom Menu							

Answer these questions for your Daily Body Check-ins

When did you say, think, agree or do something even though you felt inside that you wanted something else for yourself?	What sensations did you notice in your body when this happened?
When did you say, think, agree or do something that was good for you, but disappointed someone else?	What sensations did you notice in your body when this happened?
When did you stay in integrity on the outside and the inside and it felt good?	What sensations did you notice in your body when this happened?
What are you noticing overall about your body's 'no' sensations?	What are you noticing overall about your body's 'yes' sensations?

At the end of your week, answer these questions

What did you do each day that energized you and set yourself up for a fabulous day?

1. _____

2. _____

3. _____

4. _____

5. _____

6. _____

7. _____

What are you grateful for this week?

What do you notice about your days this week compared to last?

WEEK FIVE
Listen to Your Preferences

"Let yourself be silently drawn by the strange pull of what you really love. It will not lead you astray."

RUMI

This week's daily action is focused on listening to your preferences. Sometimes we aren't even aware we have them, but we do. It's just a matter of slowing down long enough to listen and that's what we'll be doing this week. Since this week starts on day 29, I'm recommending that you extend this practice into a regular part of your ongoing life. (Sneaky, eh?) Give it a try and I'm sure that you'll love the results!

Synthetic vs. True Pleasure

When you hear the phrase, "survival of the fittest," can you feel the energy of struggle embedded into it? It makes me want to swing back the other way and focus on what is fun! Humans are wired for pleasure, as well as survival. At our core, we are pleasure seeking beings. I remember seeing a painting from a different era in which adults from an entire community were playing alongside the children in a field. It made me wonder "What happened to all the fun???" Nicole Daedone says that women in the western world have what she calls "Pleasure Deficit Disorder." We're hustling and working hard,

---

investing a lot of effort into our lives and dreams, but lacking some very basic enjoyment that ideally would accompany everything we are doing. Instead, so many women are running around getting a lot accomplished, but are completely depleted in vitamin "P" (pleasure).

What makes this worse it that when we are low on vitamin P, we accept pleasure substitutes. Synthetic pleasure comes in many forms, such as eating sugar as a replacement for true sweetness in life, reading or watching movies about people having fun so that we can live vicariously through them, or spending hours on social media watching videos and attempting to 'connect,' only to walk away feeling more isolated and depleted.

Screw that!

As women who are fully empowered, it's our right and duty to soak up as much real and sacred pleasure as we can. It's like fuel that lights our flame. And that flame fuels passion and creativity, energizing and connecting us to our core, carrying us through discomfort and elation to see us realize our dreams and desires. Others can light their flame from us as well, so it's not just something good for us but rather something that is good for everyone around us. You know that saying, "If momma ain't happy, ain't nobody happy!" It's true. As women we set the tone and others naturally harmonize around us. It's been said that our children (or those we care about) can only be as happy as we are, no more. By no longer accepting substitutes and making pleasure a priority, we're returning ourselves and everyone we interact with to our fundamental roots.

We've strayed from being in touch with our fundamental desires, whether it's for fresh air when it's stuffy inside, for sunshine when you've been inside all day, or for warmth when you realize you're shivering cold. So how do we get to back to pleasure and resolve this cultural epidemic? We start by noticing our preferences. It's truly that simple.

It's up to you to do your part. I'm counting on you. The world is counting on you. We need a pleasure infusion, stat! So right now, before you finish reading this, take a moment to set your timer to go off once each hour... go ahead, I'll wait while you do it.

Each time the timer goes off, ask yourself this question: "What would I prefer?" And then, if it's within your ability to give it to yourself, do so. If not, congratulate yourself for taking the time to stop and notice! The main thing here is to stop for a moment to recognize your preference and begin to accommodate them. Go ahead, give yourself more sweetness in life.

Now, list 20 things that you love

1. _____
2. _____
3. _____
4. _____
5. _____
6. _____
7. _____
8. _____
9. _____
10. _____
11. _____
12. _____
13. _____
14. _____
15. _____
16. _____
17. _____
18. _____
19. _____
20. _____

That's a great start! Now, let's begin to make sure this is a habit. Anytime that you need to re-energize yourself, you can look to the list above and choose something that can spark your enthusiasm and get you reconnected to the flow of energy available to you.

Week Five	29	30	31	32	33	34	35
Power Pose & Walk							
Gratitude							
Body Check-in							
Preference Practice							

Note your observations each day below and review them at the end of the week...

1.   What did you find out about what you prefer?

2.   Was there a theme? If so, what was it?

3.   What is the first step to integrating even more time like this into your life?

Answer these questions for your Daily Body Check-ins

When did you say, think, agree or do something even though you felt inside that you wanted something else for yourself?	What sensations did you notice in your body when this happened?
When did you say, think, agree or do something that was good for you, but disappointed someone else?	What sensations did you notice in your body when this happened?
When did you stay in integrity on the outside and the inside and it felt good?	What sensations did you notice in your body when this happened?
What are you noticing overall about your body's 'no' sensations?	What are you noticing overall about your body's 'yes' sensations?

CHAPTER 8
Ending Your Sabbatical

"We shall not cease from exploration, and the end of all our exploring will be to arrive where we started and know the place for the first time."

T.S. ELIOT

Congratulations, you did it – high five!

You did it, you navigated through discomfort, uncertainty, social conditioning, inner and outer doubt and various complexities of modern life to arrive here at the end of your sabbatical. When I stop to consider your courage and your commitment, and how they're benefiting you, your family and the world around you, my heart swells.

Sit with me for a moment. Let's take time to savor what you've experienced.

Feel the new state of being, the confidence in every cell of your body. Spread your arms out and let the spaciousness you gave yourself be felt in every fiber of your being. Allow yourself to breathe once more, very deeply, and feel those aspects of yourself you reclaimed deep down in your bones. Take another breath to acknowledge your appreciation for the core you found - that inner strength, your inner authority.

Phenomenal job, high five, celebratory hug, huge smile and fist bump!

Now let's reflect back to the beginning to see how far you've come and gather those nuggets of wisdom you found along the way. **Don't skip these questions. Your goldmine of perspective is waiting for you to recognize and claim it.** You're the only one who can do it and if you skip this section it could be lost forever. You're worth the time and attention here!

Take a quick look back at the preparation steps you completed in Chapter 4 and contrast them with where you are now by answering the following questions:

What is different?

What is working well?

What would you like to improve?

What did you learn during your sabbatical?

What are you taking with you beyond the sabbatical?

What did you learn about yourself?

What do you notice about your energy levels?

What do you notice about your connection with your inner knowing?

How have those around you benefited from you prioritizing yourself?

What aspects of this experience will you be carrying forward to be part of your daily practice?

If you could have one question about this experience answered right now, what would it be?

I'd love to hear how the sabbatical went for you and have the opportunity to answer any outstanding questions you might have. If you're willing to share your answers, you can post them in the community group or even send them to me directly by completing the feedback form on the website at www.christidaniels.com/goodies. Hearing about your experience would feed my soul. You can also submit questions at the same location. There is a chance that your question and answer will be shared within the larger community, so please submit it with the broader intention that it assists you and anyone else who might have the same question.

As you reintegrate into your more "normal" life outside of the sabbatical, be easy on yourself. Any kind of change is stressful, even change that is positive and desired still comes with some tension. Life after this break will be different than before. You're a different person, you're more clear about who you are, what you want and what conditions nourish you. As you get back to regular life, you'll probably discover some situations, approaches and things that worked well in the past no longer serve you. This is good, you're growing and with that comes change, it's inevitable. The advantage you now have is that you're in touch with who you are and can navigate that change in a way that's true to you. You've eliminated some of the friction that occurred in the past from being incongruent with yourself, and that alone will reduce the level of stress you experience internally.

I remember when I came back to the 'real' world after that summer in the tent. I found that while my inner knowing had increased by enormous amounts, attempting to communicate this to another person in words was incredibly challenging. I found myself wanting the other person to 'get it' by osmosis, rather than the laborious task of putting my knowing and thoughts into words. It was odd to watch all of this happen internally, but I did just that, I noticed without judgement. It felt like an incredible experiment playing out before my eyes. You will have your own unique and interesting experience of reintegration and I encourage you to recognize it as the lifelong process it is. **We are all students growing, experimenting, noticing and seeking to identify what works.** Each time you choose to take a break and then come back, you'll see life with fresh eyes and if you could take one thing away from this experience, I hope this is the perspective that you've gained: to be easy with yourself, to look upon yourself and your life with a sense of wonder and awe as it unfolds.

You also might have discovered that rather than a sabbatical, what you've experienced during this time is something you want to claim as your new normal. Many of my clients have seen no distinct end to their sabbatical, it's simply a new way of operating in the world and only the beginning of them molding and shaping a new life for themselves that nourishes and supports who they are. This is what happened with my own modern sabbatical, I simply considered the changes I made to be my new way of operating and continued from there to create more and more congruence in my life.

Regardless of whether or not either of these approaches reflect your experience, by simply being kind to yourself, showing compassion and respect for whatever is showing up during your reintegration, you'll find your way, a way that's true to and honoring of you.

CONCLUSION

---

*"Life is large, but most of us don't take up nearly
the space the universe intended for us. We take up
this wee space 'round our toes, which is why when you
see somebody in the full flow of their humanity,
it's remarkable. They're at least a foot bigger in
every direction than normal human beings, and
they shine, they gleam, they glow. It's like they
swallowed the moon."*

SIRI LIV MYHROM

One of the most valuable aspects of creating a regular schedule for syncing up with your inner wisdom is that you get to step outside of the flow of your daily life and into a state of being rather than a state of doing. Whether it be during a lunch break on a park bench, a brisk walk outside, visiting with a friend, or journaling your thoughts, these moments of reflection are priceless. They create a space for us to hear ourselves more clearly and connect with our desires more deeply. As one last recommendation, I'd ask you to set aside a regular time on your calendar committed to an appointment with yourself. When you do this consistently at a regular time, you're able to leverage the rhythm of connection, allowing for a greater flow of ideas, insights and possibilities.

I've discovered that I work best when I collaborate with someone else and I'm less likely to skip the time if I have it scheduled with someone who's depending on me to be there. For the last five years, I've had regularly scheduled sessions with my coach. And while you might not choose to include someone else in your inner wisdom time, you can still consider your time through the lens of my favorite metaphor for coaching and mentoring sessions, which is the air traffic control tower.

As you're going through daily life, you're responding to and taking in information at the street level. It's busy, there's a lot of traffic, noise and distraction. If you're not clear about where you're going, it can be easy to get swept up in someone else's priority and find yourself off track, missing a turn, under estimating the time it takes to go from one place to another, wandering around uncertain about where you even want to go. However, when you connect with your inner wisdom it's like climbing up rungs of a ladder to the top of an air traffic control tower. With this higher level of perspective, you can see your life from a broader view. You can recognize the flight paths of people and projects, and whether or not there's a collision in sight or if things will overlap or be happening in parallel. You can sense what adjustments will be needed, you can recognize new things on the horizon, you can hear your inner wisdom because in this space, there's only a distant hum of the traffic of life below. Your inner authority is loud and clear. Here you can make choices that nourish you and cultivate the kind of life that your soul desires. You can relish in and celebrate your accomplishments, both inner and outer, and you can reflect on and claim those nuggets of wisdom. You can say exactly what is on your mind without worrying about repercussions.

As I mentioned early in the book, there's a power to doing this kind of work with other trusted companions on the path. If you have someone who's gifted as a listener, she or he can lovingly hold space and be there to listen deeply for the desire under your words and act as your mirror, reflecting back to you so you can tune in and listen for yourself. They can assist you in recognizing mistaken beliefs that have been keeping you from following your soul's desires and reframe them through the lens of your conditioning, protective armor and/ or cultural expectations. To help you liberate yourself from them and see who you are without those filters, to hone back into what is true to you, and take steps to honor that and your soul's desires.

Then you can climb back down to street level to navigate all the complexities of modern life with more confidence, joy, and ease, and less stress, because you've rooted yourself in self-awareness, deep self-trust and exquisite self-care.

Your sabbatical was a version of this, and your regularly scheduled inner wisdom time will give you the opportunity to continue with this perspective. Being connected to your core you can navigate the unknown and everything else that will come your way. Listening to your inner wisdom will guide you through the expression of your soul's desires and realizing your dreams.

Connection.

With your inner wisdom.

Connection.

With others.

And in my mind's eye, I can see you. You're a trailblazer. You're blazing as a brilliantly beautiful light across the sky, your words and essence captured for all time, your conviction on behalf of your soul's desires, your commitment to standing for yourself and in that also taking a stand for all of humanity.

I'm in awe of you.

It's my deepest desire that through reading this book, taking the sabbatical and experimenting with the daily actions you have arrived back where you started, but this time reflecting back on yourself and your life with fresh eyes, and a soft, accepting and loving heart.

I would love to think of myself as cupid, but rather than matching you up with some other mate, I hope this experience has nudged you to see and fall in love with yourself. To be so full of yourself, so connected with your inner wisdom and so grateful for this experience of life that you're willing to venture out of the safety of your comfort zone and stretch yourself out into the great unknown often and with enthusiasm, just to see what is possible for you.

When you are meeting your own needs at the highest levels, you have so much more to give to those you love. Everything you give to yourself, you're also giving to humanity.

Thank you seems hardly enough. You have the depth of my appreciation for being willing to be unabashedly you.

I can't wait to see you flashing your brilliance around!

Christi

ABOUT THE AUTHOR

Christi Daniels is a Self-fulfillment Mentor for bright, heart-centered, and driven women who've lost touch with their dreams and desires. With her *Self-Full Living™ Framework*, she empowers clients to navigate the complexities of modern life with less stress and more joy. Christi transitioned to this work after surviving 16 years of harsh spin-cycle demands in the corporate world and life as a single parent. She brings a unique understanding of the importance of deep self-trust and exquisite self-care. Christi's innovative approach is based on personal experience, cutting-edge research, timeless wisdom and practical application. The *Self-Full Living™ Framework* provides a map for finding your way back to your inner wisdom, reconnecting with your dreams, and emerging as a clearer, more confident and energized you.

Find out more and start your path to
exquisite self-care at www.christidaniels.com.

ACKNOWLEDGEMENTS

The gratitude in my heart could fill an entire book, but that's not the book you chose to read, so this is my attempt to thank those without whom this one wouldn't have been written. My words aren't effective enough to convey the level of gratitude I feel, but if you could feel inside my heart of hearts and check in with your heart, you might be able to feel it come across the page.

Mom and Dad, you gave me so much more than I ever could acknowledge and accept, and I'm incredibly grateful and honored to be your daughter. Brian, Krystal and Bryce, your kindness and love in times of crisis is a debt that can never be repaid and my gratitude and love for you run deep. Hailey, Brett and Avery, you were so brave and strong during those years of turmoil while everything was unraveling. I love you deeply and while I wish I could go back and take away the pain, disconnection and challenges, I know that each of you have grown into who you are because of them. You are beautiful, strong, powerful and brilliant. May your inner truth always be your guide.

Eric Huber, you have my unwavering love. I'm eternally grateful for your confidence in me, your love, for always being there for me and for wielding your modern day swords (websites, words, and beautiful graphic design) to bring to life and clearly communicate in seconds what has been waiting in my heart of hearts to be expressed for decades. Brett Pitts, you following your inner truth despite external pressures inspires me to up-level my own practice. Mary Lightheart, your constant love, belief in me and support helped when I forgot to believe in myself. DJ Sie, your wise woman guidance and business coaching so brilliantly held the space for me to weather many personal and professional storms, and unravel the complex web of ideas and interests to arrive at the core of them with clarity of mind and purpose. Kristy Wolfenbarger, for the first words to describe this work, your willingness to be interviewed and for inspiring me with your transparency and devotion to those you love. Dreamcrafters, for a safe, creative and productive space to brainstorm, explore ideas and gain immediate feedback. Bonnie O'Boyle, for being the muse and catalyst for the class and for inspiring me through your example of what can be accomplished when we take a *Sabbatical from "Yes." Self-Full Living*™ mentor clients and class participants, you inspire me with your courage and it's truly the honor of a lifetime to walk alongside you as you return to yourself. Kim Hodous, for providing loving, kick-ass guidance, support, belief in me and for editing the initial draft – I bow to you, sister! Parrish Wilson, you are a Michelangelo of manuscripts, able to see the potential in this draft and deftly sculpt and shape it to release a beautiful final form. Your guidance, skill and wordprints are all over this book and it would not have such depth, clarity and heart if it weren't for you. I'm eternally grateful.

And to friends, believers and guides, without whom I wouldn't have made it this far on my path, and for whom I am forever grateful and continuously learning with: Barbara Sher and the gang from the 2010 Saluda, N.C. Write-Speak Retreat, Glenda Royal, Chrysi Black, Annette Olsen, Steven Kraghmann, Joeaux Robey, Sheila Key, Alison Nail, Alisa Hudson, Stephen Parker, Marilyn Harper, Jennifer Hough and the *Born to Fly* study group. Last, but not least to the women who have inspired me and so many of us to live self-fully: Iyanla Vanzant, Oprah Winfrey, Cheryl Richardson, Lucia Capacchione, Elizabeth Gilbert, Dr. Clarissa Pinkola Estés and Barbara Stanny.

NOTES AND SOURCES

HOW TO USE THIS BOOK

Self-Full Living™ . . . : Self-Full Living™ program. Web. 23 June 2016. <http://www.christidaniels.com/self-full-living-group/>.

INTRODUCTION

One might expect . . . : ""The Supergirl Dilemma." T H E S U P E R G I R L D I L E M M a (n.d.): n. pag. The Supergirl Dilemma. A Nationwide Survey of School-Age Children Conducted for Girls Incorporated® by Harris Interactive® The Supergirl Dilemma Girls Grapple with the Mounting Pressure of Expectations SUMMARY FINDINGS ®. Web. 23 June 2016. <http://www.girlsinc-monroe.org/styles/girlsinc/defiles/The%20Supergirl%20Dilemma~Summary%20Findings~low%20res.pdf>.

The way that girls and boys . . . : Heldman, Caroline .. "Watch "The Sexy Lie: Caroline Heldman at TEDxYouth@SanDiego" Video at TEDxTalks." TEDxTalks. Tedx, 22 Jan. 2013. Web. 01 Sept. 2015. <http://tedxtalks.ted.com/video/The-Sexy-Lie-Caroline-Heldman-a>.

If girls grow up to be women . . . : MailOnline, Bianca London for. "The Video That Will Make Every Busy Woman Rethink Her Lifestyle: Elderly Ladies Reveal What They'd Do Differently If They Were Young Again (and Their Responses Will Make You Question Everything) ." Mail Online. Associated Newspapers, 25 Aug. 2015. Web. 01 Sept. 2015. <http://www.dailymail.co.uk/femail/article-3209902/The-video-make-woman-rethink-entire-life.html>.

> Ranscombe, Sian .. "British Women and the 'Cult of Never Good Enough'" The Telegraph. Telegraph Media Group, 26 Aug. 2015. Web. 01 Sept. 2015. <http://www.telegraph.co.uk/beauty/body/80-per-cent-British-women-dont-feel-good-enough/>.

> Davis, Linsey, and Enjoli Francis. "'Most Stressed Out' in U.S.? Middle-Aged Women Have Lowest Well-Being, Study Finds." ABC News. ABC News Network, 27

July 2011. Web. 23 June 2016. <http://abcnews.go.com/Health/MindMoodNews/stressed-us-middle-age-women-lowest-study-finds/story?id=14174138>.

We need to rethink our . . . : Sandberg, Sheryl. "On Mother's Day." Sheryl Sandberg. N.p., 6 May 2016. Web. 23 June 2016. <https://www.facebook.com/sheryl/posts/10156819553860177>.

When successful women like . . . : Sandberg, Sheryl. "On Mother's Day." Sheryl Sandberg. N.p., 6 May 2016. Web. 23 June 2016. <https://www.facebook.com/sheryl/posts/10156819553860177>.

CHAPTER 2

Fabulous coach . . . : Sie, Deborah. "Deborah Sie." Linked in. N.p., n.d. Web. 23 June 2016. <https://www.linkedin.com/in/deborah-sie-264a3610>.

There is a term used . . . : Rosenthal, Joshua. "Joshua Rosenthal's Bio-Individuality Is Scientifically Proven." Institute for Integrative Nutrition. Institute for Integrative Nutrition, 10 July 2015. Web. 01 Sept. 2015. <http://www.integrativenutrition.com/blog/2015/07/joshua-rosenthal-s-bio-individuality-is-scientifically-proven>

CHAPTER 3

A recent survey done by . . . : Eccles, Louise. "The Guilty-all-the-time Generation: How 96% of Women Feel Ashamed at Least Once a Day." Mail Online. Associated Newspapers, 28 Dec. 2010. Web. 23 June 2016. <http://www.dailymail.co.uk/femail/article-1342075/The-guilty-time-generation-How-96-women-feel-ashamed-day.html>.

The female brain . . . : Lapowsky, Issie. "Guilty as Charged: Women Feel More Guilt than Men, Study Says." NY Daily News. N.p., 11 Mar. 2010. Web. 23 June 2016. <http://www.nydailynews.com/life-style/guilty-charged-women-feel-guilt-men-study-article-1.174934>.

For example . . . : "A Woman's Nation Pushes Back from the Brink: Executive Summary." The Shriver Report A Woman's Nation Pushes Back from the Brink Executive Summary Comments. N.p., 11 Jan. 2014. Web. 23 June 2016. <http://shriverreport.org/a-womans-nation-pushes-back-from-the-brink-executive-summary-maria-shriver/>.

Suze Orman . . . : Orman, Suze .. "Suze Orman Quote." A-Z Quotes. A-Z Quotes, n.d. Web. 01 Sept. 2015. <http://www.azquotes.com/quote/1050949>.

Marianne Williamson . . . : Williamson, Marianne. "Marianne Williamson Quotes." Marianne Williamson Quotes (Author of A Return to Love). Good Reads, n.d. Web. 01 Sept. 2015. <http://www.goodreads.com/author/quotes/17297.Marianne_Williamson>.

Live True to You . . . : "Live True to You." https://www.facebook.com/groups/livetruetoyou/

CHAPTER 4

Before you know it . . . : Richardson, Cheryl, and Jessica Ortner. "Cheryl Richardson - 2012 Tapping World Summit." YouTube. YouTube, n.d. Web. 01 Sept. 2015. <https://www.youtube.com/watch?v=zDJW_FNJgt0>.

Nothing has . . . : Jung, C. G. "A Quote by C.G. Jung." Goodreads. N.p., n.d. Web. 01 Sept. 2015. <http://www.goodreads.com/quotes/47721-nothing-has-a-stronger-influence-psychologically-on-their-environment-and>.

Elizabeth Gilbert . . . : Gilbert, Elizabeth .. "A Quote from Committed." Goodreads. Viking, n.d. Web. 01 Sept. 2015. <https://www.goodreads.com/quotes/682175-if-i-as-a-beneficiary-of-that-exact-formula>.

While we're reflecting on loss . . . : Estés, Clarissa Pinkola. "Chapter 1 The Howl: Resurrection of the Wild Woman." Women Who Run with the Wolves: Myths and Stories of the Wild Woman Archetype. New York: Ballantine, 1995. 25-29. Print.

CHAPTER 5

When you know what drains . . . : Rubin, Hillary .. "#8 Feed Your Bandwidth with Coach Hillary Rubin | Adria DeCorte." Adria DeCorte. Feed Your Hustle Podcast, 17 Apr. 2015. Web. 01 Sept. 2015. <http://www.adriadecorte.com/hillary-rubin-honor-your-bandwidth/>.

CHAPTER 7

One of the reasons . . . : 111   Peterson, Deborah. "Oprah Winfrey:." Stanford Graduate School of Business. N.p., n.d. Web. 01 Sept. 2015. <http://www.gsb.stanford.edu/insights/oprah-winfrey-align-your-personality-your-purpose>.

Clarity comes from . . . : 113   Forleo, Marie. "Why You'll Never Find Your Passion." RSS. N.p., n.d. Web. 01 Sept. 2015. <http://www.marieforleo.com/2014/04/find-your-passion/>.

Why two minutes . . . : Cuddy, Amy J.C. "Your Body Language Shapes Who You Are." Amy Cuddy:. TED, 01 June 2012. Web. 01 Sept. 2015. <http://www.ted.com/talks/amy_cuddy_your_body_language_shapes_who_you_are?language=en>.

Your body . . . : DesMaisons, Kathleen. Potatoes Not Prozac: Simple Solutions for Sugar Sensitivity. New York: Simon & Schuster Paperbacks, 2008. Print.

My morning . . . : Tharp, Twyla, and Mark Reiter. The Creative Habit: Learn It and Use It for Life: A Practical Guide. New York: Simon & Schuster, 2003. Print.

The most meaningful lesson . . . : Moorjani, Anita. Dying to Be Me: My Journey from Cancer, to near Death, to True Healing. Carlsbad, CA: Hay House, 2012. Print.

Nicole Daedone . . . : "Nicole Daedone: Pleasure Deficit Disorder." YouTube. YouTube, n.d. Web. 01 Sept. 2015. <https://www.youtube.com/watch?v=Z8vK7Z5z3N0>.

Just a little . . . : Banks, Elizabeth M. "Video: Just a Little Heart Attack." Go Red For Women Just a Little Heart Attack Comments. Go Red For Women, 22 May 2013. Web. 01 Sept. 2015. <https://www.goredforwomen.org/about-heart-disease/symptoms_of_heart_disease_in_women/just-a-little-heart-attack/>.

CONCLUSION

Life is large . . . : Myhrom, Siri Liv. "To Be Yourself Completely: The Collective Grief of Losing Prince." On Being. On Being, 01 May 2016. Web. 23 June 2016. <http://www.onbeing.org/blog/to-be-yourself-completely-the-collective-grief-of-losing-prince/8640>.

Access the bonus materials
for *Sabbatical from "Yes"* at
www.christidaniels.com/goodies